THE COSSACK WAR
AGAINST POLAND
1648-1651

By Pierre Chevalier
Translated by G.F.Nafziger

THE COSSACK WAR AGAINST POLAND 1648-1651

By Pierre Chevalier
Translated by G.F.Nafziger

Originally Published:
Paris
Frederic, H. Scheurleer
1667

This edition:

THE NAFZIGER COLLECTION

2017

Cover Design by Dr. G.F.Nafziger
Translated by Dr. G.F.Nafziger
Cover: Tartar warrior

First Nafziger edition (C) 2015
First Published by Winged Hussar Publishing, LLC © 2017

Printed in the United States of America

ISBN 978-1-9454301-9-0
LCN

We are interested in hearing from authors with book ideas.

Published by The Nafziger Collection, Inc.
PO Box 1522, West Chester, OH 45069-1522
E-mail: Drnafziger@yahoo.com
On-line Catalog: http://www.nafzigercollection.com/

Published in conjunction with Winged Hussar Publishing, LLC
https: //www.wingedhussarpublishing.com

DEDICATION

To the Count de Bregy
Counselor to the King

In His Councils, Lieutenant General
In His Armies, and Previously
His Ambassador to Poland, Sweden, and
Other States in Northern Germany

MONSIEUR,

Having passed from the depths of Russia to France, Khmelnytsky has been consulted and advised to address himself to you, sir, who can give a more certain witness of his valor and that of his Cossacks, to which you were almost an eyewitness, during your Embassy to Poland; in which, your wonderful qualities, as well as the character of this illustrious task, you have acquired the good graces and particular confidence of the deceased King Władysław, you saw their war begun and know all the motives and secrets of it. You have engaged, also, sir, a number of these adventurers to serve in the infantry, which you raised for the King's service, in Poland, and which you had serve in Flanders where their faults were taken advantage of by your enemies, not having learned the discipline of the French armies long enough, to fortify their natural bravery. And I, who guided them for a second time in this land, that they have no recourse to any other protection than to yours, to make public so many wonderful acts, which they are content to execute, without taking any care to record them for posterity, or to relate them to other nations. They have left to me, sir, the liberty of dedicating to you their history most readily, as it is the only gratification they have made to their historiography, feeling themselves well-compensated for this work, giving them the opportunity to make to you a solemn and authentic presentation of their inviolable zeal, with which he gave throughout his life.

Monsieur

Your most humble and
very obedient servant,
Pierre Chevalier

Pierre Chevalier

FORWARD
to the Readers

Having made a collection of details I have learned about the Cossacks during my voyages to Poland, I wrote my memoires, which I never thought would see the light of day. A curious individual had, after my return, obliged me to give him a copy, which subsequently passed into the hands of many others, and one finally did me the honor of insisting for a collection of my diverse travel accounts. Even though some errors slipped in during the printing, quite pardonable as the printer did not know the Polish or Ruthenian languages, I was unable to refuse some of my friends, who knew that I was the author of this work, to give it to the public, and they believed that I would do it with more precision. I have added to it a discourse on the Little Tartars and the history of the war between the Cossacks and Poland in the year 1648, which they claim started in 1652. I had put an abridged account of this war in the discourse on the Cossacks, but I have removed it, this time to eliminate the boredom of repetition, so that I might present it in greater detail in this history. It would be better, if I used more substantial memoirs, but it contains all that is known in Poland. It has been 10 years and everything in Poland has been overthrown by new wars, no less terrible than that of the Cossacks. So no one has written it. Thus, if the reader, should travel there, they will be informed about some of the relations we have had with the Cossacks and Tartars, who have not occupied themselves in writing their history, and do not find it strange that anyone has said so little about them. This light treatment does not provide a bigger picture of the issues, and it is necessary to leave it to someone with a more skillful and better informed to paint a more perfect picture. Whatever happens, we can always praise the century where we know more about foreign nations than the Romans did, at least as they appear in the histories that they have left us, even though they had more advantages than we, since the Romans subjugated almost all of them, and could, as a result, better know them.

There are circumstances in this history, which may displease the reader. One will note here an unusual manner of fighting a war and of combat; acts of bravery which belong in a novel, armies that will remind us of what was written about the Huns, Goths, Vandals, Persians, and Turks; and that which is more marvelous, a single man who rose above the others, who moved all the great machines, and who spread terror in a kingdom, which all the powers of Christianity and even the Turks, had been unable to shake. In a word, a Cromwell reproduced in a Russian, who was no less ambitious, brave, and political than that of Englishmen.

The proper names of men and of cities where the Slavic orthography is obscure and this multiplicity of consonants, which envelop the vowels, are difficult for some; but I have mispronounced these words a little so as to not give them a significant different from their nature, or to make them more so. It would be absurd to distort the pronunciation to our words for strangers who have no facility to pronounce them than for us to add or remove some letters. I know well that several ancient and modern historians have acted otherwise, but they have not done well and it is desired that they had left complete the proper names of men, lands, and cities in the foreign histories that they have written. The changes that they have produced, or planned, or perhaps by ignorance, have so well disguised them that one does not have the time to decrypt them. In addition I do not know if my work shall be approved, since has been done from that which I was asked to make public. I shall be sufficiently compensated for the little time that it has cost me, if I know that it will be well received. This would excite me to produce another on the subject of the affairs of Poland, of greater breadth, which is well advanced, and may see the light of day, if time permits.

NOTES ON THIS EDITION

The original title of this work was *Histoire de la guerre des Cosaques contre la Pologne* [*History of the War of the Cossacks Against Poland*]. I have modified the title slightly to make its subject more understandable to the modern reader who is not familiar with this obscure war.

The translation of this work presented some unusual difficulties. It is difficult to discuss a translation of a 17th century work without speaking about the evolution of the French language. The Académie française, which is the arbiter of the French language, was created by Cardinal Richlieu in 1635, a bare 32 years before this work was published. The Académie was charged with establishing a standardized spelling for French words, standard definitions for those words, and fixing the grammar in which those words are used. Sadly, that standardization was far from universal even one hundred years later, so as I worked through this work I found it to be a chaos of phonetic spellings hung on the author's perception of proper grammar. A minor issue was the lower case "s" being written as "f." Added to this "u" and "v" were interchangeable. The "ê" was in its original of "es," but appearing as "ef" and this randomly replaced "é" and "è." As a result of the author's unusual grammar and a propensity towards tremendously long sentences, I have found it necessary to be flexible in my translation of this work.

I also need to point out that there were words that are not in the current French dictionary or even the lexicon of *Chrestomathie des Prostateurs française du quatorzième au siezième siècle* (Geneva: Cherbuliez, 1862), which contains a collection of 14th to 16th century French words and their translations. Because of this I was unable to completely translate some passages and had to work around the obsolete terms with my best guess.

Where possible I have tried to use the proper spelling of the names of the people in this work and the proper spellings of the city names. In some cases they are unknown and unknowable, especially when run through pre-standardized French. However, it should be noted that the author discusses this problem in his introduction. I have kept his spellings intact with few exceptions where I could identify the historical figure or the city involved.

One will also note that many of the Polish generals had titles in the original that are French. Where possible I have tried to convert them to Polish terms. The French and Poles had a long relationship, that there were alliances and even dynastic marriages. Indeed, the King, Stanisław Leszczyński's daughter was married to Louis XV and after his exile he was made the Duke of Lorraine and died in France.

-George Nafziger

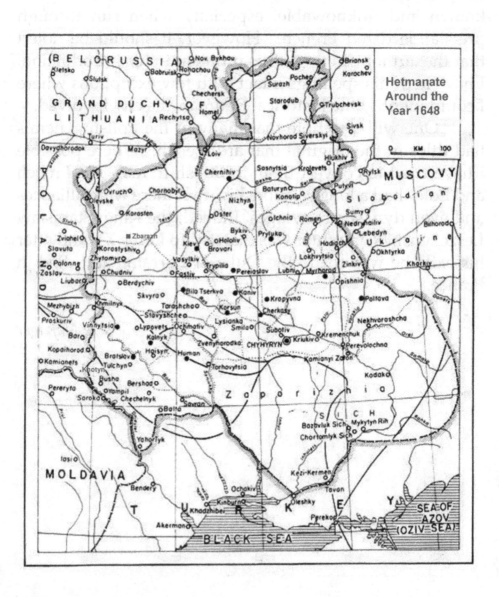

Hetmanate Around the Year 1648

0   KM   100

THE LANDS,
Customs, Government, Origin, and Religion of the Cossacks

The name of "Cossack" was given to them because of the agility and the skill with which they penetrated into the most terrible and difficult places, such as the mouth of the Dnieper, in order to make war against the Turks and the Little Tartars. "Cosa" in Polish means "goat."

Back in the time of Sigismund I, The Elder, it was volunteers from the frontiers of Russia, Volhynia, Podolia, and other provinces of Poland who flocked, as they have done since, to go pirating on the Black Sea where they often gained considerable success and a rich booty from the Turkish galleys, which they encountered on this sea, and on the incursions that they made on the shores of Anatolia, where they frequently pillaged and sacked entire cities, such as Trebizond and Sinope. With the same boldness, they occasionally advanced within a few leagues of Constantinople taking prisoners and booty. When the campaign ended each of these adventurers returned home, after being given a rendezvous at the islands and reefs of the Dnieper so that they could assemble in the spring and to return to their raids.

King Stephen Bathory, to whom Poland owes many beautiful laws, considered the service that he drew from these corsairs as a sort of militia and guard on the frontiers of Russia and Podolia, which were always exposed to the incursions of the Tartars, gave them the city and territory of Trakhtemyriv on the Dnieper, to serve them as a *place d'armes*. He created a general for them to whom he gave the power to elect the subordinate officers that he needed to serve under him, and gave them privileges and immunities, in addition to their pay. He added 2,000 cavalry to the Cossack infantry for the subsistence of which he designated a quarter part of all the revenues of the domain, calling them "quartani," and this was corrupted into "quartiani."[1]

These forces, were established for guarding of the frontier, assured it against Tartar incursions as the deserted land beyond the cities of Braslav, Bar, and Kiev were beginning to be populated and a number of cities and fortresses were constructed, each of which produced colonies in the neighboring provinces.

This regulated militia was always maintained and provided good services to Poland and, without comparison, acted more effectively than before. However, being dispersed it could not act in concert. Despite this, its union was advantageous when it came to resisting the Tartars as it covered the frontier, but this also frequently raised army of rabble which was found to be ruinous and damaging, in a short time, to this Republic. In effect, the Cossacks felt themselves so important that they soon did not wish to receive orders from their superiors, no longer recognizing the Polish lords who they had followed. Their first rebellion was in 1587, under John Podkova, their general, who was captured and beheaded. In 1596, King Sigismund III had prohibited them from making their accustomed raids on the Black Sea, as a result of the complaints that he had received from the Great Lord [Sultan]. They stopped those raids, but turned on Russia and Lithuania where they per-

---

[1]These were the part of the paid Crown forces.

petrated horrible ravages, under the command of General Nalyvaiko. In vain, orders were sent for them to disarm and return to their houses, but they scorned those orders and drew closer to their chief, so as to resist the Polish army, which Polish Hetman[2] Żółkiewski was obliged to lead against them, to stop them. They waited for him before the city of Bila Cerkva and successfully fought against the Poles. However, Żółkiewski, who was a great captain, pressed them closely and pushed them into a disadvantageous position, forcing them to surrender. Nalyvaiko was lashed to death, meeting an end parallel to that of his predecessor.

In 1637, the Cossacks revolted again, but with as little success as before. The cause of their uprising was the nobility's acquisition or obtaining by gift lands that were on the frontier in the locations designated for the quarters of this militia, and these nobles sought to augment their revenues by subjecting their new subjects, to the same degree as the other provinces of Poland were held. These new land holders persuaded King Władysław and the Republic, that it was necessary to chastise the insolence of the Cossacks. They sought to impose their yoke on the peasants. To this end they sought to build a fort in a location called Kudak, on the Dnieper. It would contain the Cossacks. It was close to the *porohi* or the reefs of this river, which made their retreat more secure. Because they initially wanted Colonel Marion François, who General Koniecpolski had left there with 200 men to build this fort, it was necessary to leave a party of these troops to winter over until it was in a solid state of defense. The Cossacks, understood the reasons for the construction of this fort, as a matter of urgency, were alarmed and assembled as large

---

[2]An Army commander appointed by the King

a force as they could. However, at a time when they had the greatest need of unity, they defied their Hetman Sava-konovicz, murdered him, and after a tumultuous discussion elected a certain Pavlyuk in his place. Pavlyuk was a man of little drive or experience. They soon paid dearly for this choice, because they were engaged by Field Hetman Potocki in the vicinity of Korsun. As they had little cavalry they were easily defeated. The fugitives were thrown into Borowitz, where Potoski besieged them and because the fortress was stripped of all munitions, they were obliged to surrender Hetman Pavlyuk. When they surrendered four of their principal officers were present. Though these four men had been promised their lives they were beheaded in Warsaw during the Diet held the next year. The Republic had not kept its word.

The loss of their generals was followed by the loss of their privileges and the fortress of Trakhtemyriv, earlier given to them by King Stephen, and finally the disbanding of their militia. In its place the King of Poland ordered his officers to produce a new force that would be more obedient.

The Cossacks did not lose courage and after these disgraces, made their last efforts to maintain their liberty.

After having suffered defeats under Hetman Potocki and finding themselves notably weakened by a series of running battles, they entrenched themselves beyond the Dnieper, on the Starcza River, where they withstood, for more than two months, several attacks by the Poles. The Poles, after losing much of their force, were obliged to sign an agreement with the Cossacks, promising that they would re-establish their privileges. The Poles also promised that the Cossack Militia[3] would be re-established,

---

[3]Registered Cossacks, recognized by the Crown and provided an allowance. The Crown capped the number of troops recognized under this designation.

with 6,000 men, under the command of a general, who would be given to them by the King of Poland. The Poles, however, did not maintain their faith and as before, when they separated, most of the Cossacks were killed or imprisoned by the soldiers of the Polish army. Their militia was not re-established, but a new force was formed where the general was frequently changed and true Cossacks were excluded.

The damage produced by this change was soon felt. The Tartars, who executed a raid two years later pushed far into the Ukraine and ravaged the territories of Pereiaslav, Korsun, and Wiśniowiec, which they had not dared to approach before the formation of the Cossacks. They returned some time later and King Władysław, who saw this militia as vital in the war he intended to make against the Tartars and Turks, contributed a great deal to their re-establishment and gave them as their Hetman, Bohdan Khmelnytsky, who the King drew from their corps and was raised to the nobility.

One can infer from this discourse that the Cossacks were a militia and not a nation as many have believed. One could very well compare them to the free archers established in France by Charles VIII, who were men chosen from all the parishes of his kingdom that were capable of bearing arms and who, at the first order of the King, would go to a rendezvous, which had been assigned to them, and who were obliged to serve in the war. This service exempted them from all charges and taxes. The Cossacks were the same, chosen and enrolled in Russia, Volhynia, and Podolia, and who had several freedoms and privileges. They equally marched where they were commanded to march. They had, as has been earlier noted, only a single city for their retreat, where their general established his residence, at the Porohis of Dnieper, from where they were called "Zaporozhian Cossacks", and by which they were distinguished from the Cossacks that come from Moscow and on the Don or Tanais.

"Porohi" is a Russian term which indicates "Peter of the Rock." This river was 50 leagues from its mouth and is crossed by rocks, which serve as a dike in the middle of its bed. It is this which renders navigation impossible and gave the Ukraine the means to enrich itself by transporting all sorts of goods to Constantinople. There are some rocky outcrops in the river, some that are six, eight, and ten feet tall and which form rapids, which the Cossacks can cross, but only at great risk in their small boats. There are thirteen of these rapids, some of which are 12-15 feet high when the waters are low. It is necessary to cross them in order to be recognized as a true Zaporozhian Cossack and to have, as a result, made a voyage in the Black Sea. This is the same with the Knights of Malta, obliged to make a caravan in order to be recognized as a true member of the brotherhood.

There are diverse islands beyond the Porohis of the Dnieper. They are seen, among others, below the Czertomelik River, surrounded by more than 10,000 others, which are dry, and others that are swampy, and all of which are covered with reeds. As a result, one cannot discern the canals that separate them. It is in this location and its many detours into which the Cossacks retreat and which they call their "*skarbniza wojskowa*," which is to say, "the treasure of the army." This is where they put all the booty that they have taken in their raids on the Black Sea. Access is so difficult and so dangerous that several Turkish galleys that pursued them into those channels were lost. This is also the location where they gather to go on their raids.

After they arrived and they elected a general from their ranks to lead and command their expedition, they work on their boats, which are 60 feet long and 10-12 feet wide. They have no keel and are a small boat made of planking that is pegged together. They have two paddles to better turn when they are obliged to flee and cover their sides with large ropes of reeds like a barrel to sustain these boats against waves. There are ordinarily 10, 12, or 15 oars on each side, which makes them faster than the Turkish galleys. They carry a merchant sail, but they use it only in good times, preferring to row when there is heavy wind. As for provisions for their cruises, they carry biscuit, which they keep in barrels and remove through a bung to the degree that they need them. With this they have a barrel of boiled millet and another of broken dough mixed with water which they mix with the millet. This serves them as food and drink simultaneously and they think it most delicious. They take neither brandy nor any strong drink.

They ordinarily assemble 5,000 to 6,000 men and after allocating about 60 to build each boat, in three weeks they have 80 to 100 ready. They put 50-60 men in each boat, armed with 5-6 fauconneau[4] and two arquebuses[5], with the necessary powder and ball. The admiral has a flag on his mast to distinguish him from the others. They sail together and very close, without touching. They wait for the end of the month to come out of the Dnieper in order to escape observation by the galleys that ordinarily stand at Ochakiv, a Turkish city at the mouth of this river. If they are spotted, the alarm spreads throughout the land and as far as Constantinople. From there couriers are sent on all the roads of Anatolia, Rumelia, and Bulgaria in order that each may hold himself on guard. However, the

---

[4]A small cannon
[5]An early rifle

diligence of the Cossacks is such that they ordinarily arrive before all the couriers that carry the news of their coming. The transit, aided by the weather and season, takes them 40 hours to reach Anatolia.

When they encounter galleys or ships, which they can discover better and at a distance, they hug the coast, as their boats draw only two and a half feet of water, approaching by night, but remaining a league or so away. Then, at midnight, they row at full force and in a moment surround and take the ship. It is not possible for a ship surrounded and attacked from all directions in this manner to defend itself. From captured vessels they take money, cannon, and all the merchandise which they can easily transport, then sink the ship since they are not able to take it away. However, if they have such an advantage over galleys and ships during the night, they can fight as well during the day. When they encounter a ship they fire their cannon and kill many of the target's crew. They fight relentlessly, having only half of their crew rowing. It is true that they can never be caught, withdrawing when they are pursued into the reeds and towards the shores, where the galleys cannot go. The Great Lord [Sultan] has frequently complained of their piracy to the King of Poland, who has never given him satisfaction, because of the constant incursions by the Tartars, against whom God cannot arouse a more formidable enemy than the Cossacks.

As for their manner of warfare on land, they are better on foot than on horse, patient, enduring, obedient to their chiefs, and extremely skillful in moving earth and entrenching themselves, not only by digging, but also with their wagons[6] , with which they march and which are so strong behind this moving entrenchment, which is abso-

---

[6] Translator: The author is describing the sort of wagon fort used by Jan Siska or the Boers' wagen laager.

lutely necessary in these desert plains, where the Tartars constantly run. A force of 1,000 Cossacks thus covered can withstand 6,000 of these infidels who never get off their horses and are stopped by a ditch or the least barricade. It would also be difficult in other lands, such as Poland, to march an army in the middle of their wagons.

The land inhabited by the Cossacks is called the Ukraine, which means "the frontier." It is all the land extending beyond the Volhynia and Podolia, and forms part of the Palatinates of Kiev and Braclav. They have become masters, in recent years, of these provinces and part of Black Russia, which they were subsequently obliged to abandon. This country extends from 51° to 48° Latitude, beyond which there are nothing but desert plains as far as the Black Sea. On one side are bounded by the Danube and on the other by the Limen or Palus Meotide. The grass that grows in this region is tall enough to conceal a man on horse with ease.

The Ukraine is a very fertile land, as are Russia and Podolia, and wherever the land is cultivated, produces all sorts of grains, which the inhabitants don't know how to use it all most of the time. Its rivers are not navigable. They have every sort of domestic beast, game, and fish as well as honey, and wax in abundance, and the wood with which they construct their houses. They only lack wine and salt, the first is sold to them by Hungary, Transylvania, Walachia, and Moldovia, as well as beer, mead, and brandy, which they make from grain and are thus very amateurish. For salt, they draw it from the salt mines of Wieliczka, near Krakow, or Pokutia, which is a region of Poland, Transylvania, and Moldavia, where most of the wells are salty, which is boiled in France, to produce a white salt. It is made in little loafs. This salt is agreeable to eat, but is not as salty as the salt from Brouage.

All the houses of this land are made of wood, as they are in Moscow and Poland. The city walls are made of earth, supported by horizontal blanks at their base, as in a cofferdam. They are resistant to fire, but also they are a better defense against cannon shots than masonry.

The principal rivers are the Dnieper, the Bug, the Dniester or Tyras, which borders Walachia, the Desna, the Ros, the Horin, the Slucz, the Ster, and several lesser rivers, the number of which reflects the goodness of the territory.

The largest cities and fortresses occupied by the Cossacks are Kiev, where there is a Palatine and a Greek Orthodox Metropolitan, Bila Tserkvo, Korsun, Starocons-tiantyniv, Bar, Cherkasy, Chyhyryn, Kudak, Yampil, the crossing over the Dniester, Braclaw, over the Bug, Palatinate, Vinnytsia, Human, Chernihiv, Pereiaslav, Lubny, Pavoloch, and Chvastov. All of these cities were well-fortified in the last few years and the Sieur de Beauplan, a French engineer, who was in the service of the deceased Grand Hetman Koniespolski and is known to the public for the two very exact maps that he created of the Ukraine, has laid out the fortifications of most of those cities. Beyond these cities, there is no village or town that has ramparts, but they are all defended by ditches to protect themselves against the incursions of the Tartars, who frequent this region.

The peasants of the Ukraine and the neighboring provinces are like slaves, like the others of Poland. They are obliged to work three or four hours a week for their lords, be it with their horses or their arms. They are, in addition to this, charged with several fees of grain and fowl for the ground that they hold, to pay the tithe (10%) of their sheep, swine, and all the fruit, and in addition a quantity of wood, and to perform various corvées. Joined to this is the very bad treatment of the Jews. Peasants living on noble lands, made stringent demands before the war to get rights to brew beer and make brandy. So, it should not be surprising that they frequently revolted and as in the last wars, they had disputed and stubbornly defended their liberty. However, this harsh slavery had given birth to all the brave Zaporozhian Cossacks, whose number has greatly increased in the past few years because of the despair into which the harshness of the nobility and Jews had thrown these frontier people, which pushed them to seek their liberty and end their miseries.

The inhabitants of the Ukraine, who are all today called Cossacks and who are proud to carry this name, are of a good height, disposition, and robust. They are liberal and little concerned about amassing goods; great lovers of their liberty, they will suffer no yoke, indefatigable, bold and brave, but great rogues, perfidious and treacherous, they occupy themselves with hunting and fishing and all that is necessary for a rustic life and for war. What is particular to them is that they prepare the best saltpeter, with which their lands abound, and much of it is sent throughout Europe, sending it to Gdansk where the Dutch and other nations buy it.

This land is greatly blighted with biting flies, which are particularly common in the east, and forces the inhabitants to sleep in a *"pollen"* which is a hut very similar to those of the soldiers who cover themselves with a cotton cloth, where the edges close, and hang a foot and a half below the mattress, in order that there is no opening left. These flies are more of a problem than the grasshoppers [locusts] that come periodically, principally when the weather is very dry.

They are pushed by an east or southeast wind from Tartary, Circassia, and Mingrelia[7] , which are almost never

---

[7]Area in Western Georgia

exempted. They come in clouds that are five or six leagues long and three or four wide, which obscures the air and in the most severe instances blocks out the sun. In places where they land, they strip the ground in two hours of the wheat that is still growing. These insects only live six months. In places where they live in autumn, they lay their eggs, each producing about 300 eggs. They hatch in the following spring, when it is dry, and become locusts. Heavy rains kill them and this is the only means of destroying this plague, or when the wind comes from the north or northwest, because it drives them towards the Black Sea. When they are born and when they are no longer strong enough to fly they enter houses and go into the beds, on the tables, on the meat such that one cannot eat it. At night they fill the roads and ground to a depth of four inches and when a wagon passes over them they emit a terrible stench.

The Russians and Cossacks suffer from a particular disease called by doctors "*plica*," and in the local language "*goschest*." Those who are attacked by it are crippled in their limbs, are paralyzed, and suffer great pain. When this passes, one night they suffer a great sweating of the head such that all their hair sticks together, then the patient feels much relieved and, after a few days, are cured of their paralysis. However, their hair remains tangled and must be cut; the humors that come from the pores of the head fall on the eyes and render them blind. This disease is deemed incurable, but Sieur de Beauplan assures us that he has cured several treating it as if it was the pox. It is thought that this disease originates in bad water or that it is a venereal disease.

The language of the Cossacks is a dialect of Polish. It is very delicate and filled with diminutives and many dainty fashions of speaking.

As to their religion, they are Greek Orthodox, which came into their land in 942 AD during the reign of Vladimir Prince of Russia. The better part of the nobility is Catholic, Lutheran, or Calvinist.[8]

---

[8]Translator: A discussion of the differences between the Catholic and Greek Orthodox religions followed at this point. It has been eliminated.

DISCOURSE ON THE
Perekop Tartars

There are two great peoples in the world who think in the same manner, who are of the same religion, and have, based on what they claim, the same origin. These are the Arabs and the Tartars. The first occupy a part of Asia and Africa and the second occupy all the regions north of the former, extending as far as Europe. Some of these people, the more civilized of the two, have cities and cultivate the sciences and arts. However, most of them live a country life or a nomadic life. They live in tents, or no other cover than the sky. They engage in little agriculture, preferring the hunt, war, or brigandage, and have no other riches than their herds.

The Tartars are divided into hordes and the Arabs into "heylas" or "cobeyles." They do not make alliances [marry] outside of their lines or blood, which produces the great resemblance that they have between them and certain facial traits that easily distinguishes them from other nations.

The Tartars, who are properly called Scythians, have not been known by that name for more than 400 years. Some authors give the source of their name from the River Tartar, while others, such as Leuvenclavius[1] , from the lands that they occupied in ancient history.

---

[1]Translator: Johannes Leunclauvis, or Johannes Löwenklau (1541 – June 1594). He studied in Wittemberg, Heidelberg, and Basel, disciple of Guillaume Xylander. He traveled extensively. He translated into Latin many Greek works. He also wrote on the relations between Livonia and Moscow (1561) and a history of the Ottoman sultans.

There are others who claim that "Tartar" is improper and a corruption; that they should be called Tartares or Totares, a Scythian word that indicates a "remainder." Supposing that these people are the remains of the 10 tribes of Israel, which Salmanazar and his predecessors took as captives into Assyria, who subsequently resolved to separate from the gentiles and moved into an uninhabited land to freely exercise their religion and observe the laws that they had misunderstood.

According to Magin, Tartary is divided into five parts. The first part is Little Tartary, or the Perekop Tartary, also called the Crimea; the second is the Asiatic Samara, which contains several hordes of Tartars that are subjects of the Grand Duke of Moscow, such as the Cheremisses, Nagais, Zauolhans, and those from Kazan and Astrakhan. The third are the Zagaray or the Land of Vzbek, or the Scythia of Mont Imaus, which extends from the banks of the Chesel, or the Iaxarte, and from Gehon of Oxe, which includes Bactria and Sogdiana. It is in this Tartary where the famous Tamerlane reigned. The fourth is Cathay or Scythia of the Imaus, commonly called the Grand Tartary, the Cham of which has since become the master of China, and the fifth is the ancient Tartary or Scythia unknown to Ptolemy, which is the most advanced of the east and north side of Asia.

The Little Tartary, also called the Chersonese Taurick, is called the Perekop Tartary after a city of that name, which is situated on the isthmus of a peninsula, which is called, in Slavic, a "dug place" because of the ditch that cuts the throat of this isthmus. It is also called Krim or Crimea, after one of its principal cities.

Its ancient inhabitants were the Taures, who gave this name to their land. Several Greek colonies were subsequently established there. Then some Tartar hordes came from the vicinity of the Caspian Sea, after having ravaged part of Asia and crossed the Volga. They captured it in about 460 AD, with the exception of some ports and Cassa, among others, which remained in the hands of the Genoese from 1266 AD to 1475 AD when Mohammed II, Emperor of the Turks, captured it.

The Chersonese Taurick was about 50 leagues long and in some places was 30 leagues wide, and in others only 1 league. However, Little Tartary extends further, including the Budziak, which is a country between the Dniester and the Dnieper, and as far as the Don or Tanais along the sea from Elle Zabache to Palus Meotides.

There are no cities or villages, however, except in the Chersonese, the rest being uncultivated, grassy plains and in which the Tartars wander about grazing their herds. They live in rolling cabins that protect them, in the winter, from the great cold and snow. Part of each group watches the herd, while the rest of them, when the rivers and swamps are frozen, occupy themselves with raids into the Ukraine and on the frontiers of Moscow.

The cities of the peninsula are primarily Perekop, called "Or" by the Tartars, where there are about 400 hearths; it is situated on the east of the isthmus, whose width is about a half league. Koslow, situated on one of the capes of the isthmus and on the Black Sea, has about 2,000 hearths, is a commercial city and belongs to the Kahn. Crim is another city belonging to the Khan, sitting on a bay that is part of the Sea of Elle Zabacche [Sea of Azov], which is almost entirely occupied by Tartars. Baciasaray, where the Khan ordinarily holds his court, has about 2,000 hearths. Almasary contains another of the Khan's palaces, which he frequently visits. When he goes there he is only accompanied by a *bourgad* of 60 to 80 hearths at most.

The places occupied by the Turks are the port of Balaclava, greatly esteemed and the destination of many ships and galleys. However, it is a *bourgad* of 100 or 200 hearths. Ingermann and Mancyp are castles with some ruined cities. However, what supports them is the considerable city of Caffa, otherwise known as Theodosia. It was, under the Genoese, a considerable mercantile city engaged in commerce with the Levant. It has since decayed considerably from its earlier condition, like the other cities that have come under Ottoman domination. However, there are still 5,000 to 6,000 hearths there. The inhabitants of this city are mainly Greeks and Italians. The rest are Genoese, Armenians, Jews, Turks, and Tartars. Most of them are Christian. There are 45 Greek, Armenian, and Latin churches in the city.

The Chersonese Taurik consists of fertile plains, forests, and mountains, producing all sorts of grains, excellent fruit, and wine. The Christians and Jews plow the land, but the Tartars use slaves to perform this task. On the whole, the Tartars prefer being shepherds or thieves. Their horses and their herds are their treasure, along with booty along with male and female slaves that they take in their raids, which they sell to Christian merchants and the Jews of Jaffa. They exchange their slaves for provisions and the merchants then take those slaves to Constantinople, Sinope, Trebizond, and other places in the Levant. They particularly like Polish women and girls which sometimes go as far as Persia and the Indies to become part of the seraglios of those lands where they are greatly esteemed. The male slaves frequently end up in Egypt where they become part of the Mamelukes. But since Selim ruined this military empire, this commerce with Egypt has ended.

The Perekop Tartars are, for the most part, of medium height, robust, with large arms, shot necks, a large face, and small eyes, which are very black and almond-shaped. They are accustomed to every sort of work and exercises from their infancy. Their mothers bathe them almost daily in salt water in order to make their bodies firmer and more impenetrable to the impurities of the air, something that is also practiced by Polish women, but they content themselves in doing it once a week. Their fathers accustom them to firing the bow and at the age of twelve or fifteen they take them with them to war.

The country Tartars are dressed in sheepskin and wear a pointed sheepskin hats. Their ordinary arms are a saber, bow, and quiver containing about 20 arrows. They make their own bows using horse tendons; their quivers are made from hide, and they bind their iron arrowheads to their arrows with hide straps. They handle their whips with skill, which is particular to them. Their whips are no longer imitated by the French and German saddle makers. They have begun to use iron weapons. All of them are armed with knives. The bridles and the saddles of their horses are made of wood and are unique to them. They use compasses to cross deserts where there is no road or beaten path. The leaders among them are dressed in multi-colored cloth, linen or cotton, mail jackets, Turkish saddles, and a more honest equipment, which they have bought from Armenian merchants or which they captured in war.

Their horses, which they call *"bacmates,"* are thin and ugly, having thick mains and long tails that fall to the ground. But nature has repaired their ugliness with a speed and ability to endure fatigue without equal. They can travel all day without being unsaddled. They are always outside, even when the ground is covered with snow, and they live on what they can find under the snow or branches and the bark of trees, pine needles, thatch, and whatever they can find.

As for the leading Tartars, they have Turkish and Arab horses and their Khan has the most beautiful harnesses.

The Tartars eat almost no bread. They eat millet which is very common among them, or to make a soup or a beverage. They also eat horse meat, which they boil when they are at rest alone or with millet. When they go to war or are on the march, they cook it or more frequently, placing the fresh meat under their saddles and eat it in that state with no seasoning other than the scum that forms on this meat, from their horses' sweat. They do not choose the fattest or the healthiest of their horses to be slaughtered, but they take those that have foundered or which are sick or lame. I have seen, among prisoners held in Poland, the Tartars butcher dead horses and divide the meat among themselves.

Because they are Muslim, wine is forbidden. Their usual drink is water or snow in winter when the rivers and streams are frozen. Sometimes they drink bouillon made of horse, with all the scum, or *breha*, which is a beverage made of boiled millet. They also drink the milk of their horses, mead, and brandy, and eat mutton, goat, and fowls. They will also eat game, as they frequently hunt, but because of their faith, they do not eat pork. One can say that, in general, they are sober and content. As for the Khan, he sets a most delicious table, is superbly housed, and lives in a magnificence worthy of his position.

Their language is similar to that of the Turks, having the same origin, but is mixed with many Persian and Arab words.

As to their customs, it is difficult to imagine a more virtuous people, because in addition to their restraint, of which I have already spoken, they are extremely sincere and faithful, there are no thieves or false witnesses among them, no injustice and no violence. They live, in a word, in a great union and perfect tranquility, but they do not see it as a crime when they ravage the lands of Christians, whom they see as infidels and abominable. Every day in Poland one see examples of the marvelous fidelity of the Tartars that are captives, not failing to return on the designated day, when they are sent out on their word to procure their liberty by arranging an exchange of Polish prisoners. They execute punctually or return without missing a moment. I have seen Polish gentlemen confiding in young Tartars that are in their service the keys to their money and their most precious possessions, but not to anyone else in their households.

These people obey a prince which they call the "*Khan*", which is to say "king." The Poles use the word "czar", which come to us from the word "caesar." It is very respected and despotic reign like almost all the Muslim princes. The Khan has the power to designate his successor, who is ordinarily his son or one of his brothers. This designated successor is called the "*galga*." The notables or the most notable of the Cham's subjects are called "*murzas*." Since Selim, Emperor [Sultan] of the Turks, to which part of the Tartars have sworn fealty, the Khans have not become tributaries, as some historians indicate. They are vassals of the Great Lord [Sultan], who as a mark of his suzerainty, send the Tartars a standard at the change of the *Khan*. The first king or *Khan* of the people, being a certain Vlan, claimed a miraculous birth. His successors were replaced a few years ago by the Girays and they now sit on the throne. The Vlan family had died out without heir, so they were replaced by the Girays.

The religion of the Perekop Tartars is Islam and their language is Turkic. Their form of government is very similar to that of the Turks. The Prime Minister of the Khan is called a Vizier, like that of the Grand Lord. They have mullahs and cadis, who render justice, for the administration of which they have no other document than the Koran, which they interpret literally.[2]

The prince's army is very large, as he gathers together all the hordes that are obedient to him or are his allies. He can mobilize 300,000 cavalry. But he has no infantry, unless there are some Janissaries, which he would obtain from Turkey for his use in a specific expedition. They maintain some garrisons in castles or strong points on the Tauric, but there are very few of these men. His largest fortress is Perekop or Or, which has only a large ditch four or five toises[3] deep and has a rampart a terrace 7-8 feet high and is 2½ toises wide. They always have a strong guard to defend the entrance to the peninsula, and a man who is the commanding governor of the hordes that lay between the Dnieper and the Danube.

The normal form of Tartar warfare is a raid. In those times of peace that they have had with their Christian neighbors there have been no attacks, even though the Khan claims tribute from the Muscovites and the Poles, which they have paid at times, when necessity obliged it, but refused on other occasions when they did not want to be subjected to infidels that they distrust.

When the Tartars wish to make their great invasions, be it Poland or Moscow, they ordinarily choose the full moon of January, when all the rivers, lakes, and marshes

---

[2]Translator: The author's discussion of how their legal system has been eliminated.

[3]Translator: A "toise" is approximately a meter.

are frozen as is the ground in the deserted plains, which is covered with snow and is easy for the horses. Each Tartar takes with him two horses for relays, or to carry his booty and his food, which are not heavily laden, carrying only a little and some pulverized meat, like the Turks, with some garlic to aid the digestion both of the cooked things that they eat and sometimes when there is no meat left while on the march. They move by valleys and covered places so as to not be seen by the Cossacks who are always in vedettes to gain news and spread the alarm of the Tartars coming through the land. What is surprising is that in the winter they camp without fire, out of fear of being discovered, and only eat the meat that their horses have under their saddles. When they arrive in the area that they have targeted, be it in the Ukraine or elsewhere, their generals detach a third of their army, which divides into other troops and go on raids, pillaging five or six leagues on the wings, while the bulk of the army remains gathered together so as to be able to fight their enemies, if they present themselves. Then when the raiders return from their pillaging, another group is sent to pillage, always observing this order, which all the troops, which travel here and there, can in a short time return to the main body. After having thus pillaged and ravaged the land for four, five, or six days, they withdraw quickly so that they are not attacked in their retreat, and having regained the deserted plains where they have a greater advantage when they fight, they stop to regain their breath and divide up the booty and prisoners.

They also make raids into Ere, but they are of only 10,000 to 12,000 men at most and frequently less. These are the Budziak Tartars, who ordinarily move in this season and pasture their herds and horses in the desert plains or where they carry off everything they encounter. This is why one cannot move in a tabor [wagon laager]⁴ without large escorts of 500 to 1,000.

The Tartars only fight in large groups of 2,000, 3,000, or 4,000 horses, or stronger still. They will not attack if they are not stronger than their prey. When pressed, they break up and scatter in small troops that the Polish and Germans, who move in closed ranks, cannot engage. While they retreat, they fire their arrows to the rear with such intensity that they fly more than one hundred paces. They rally after a quarter of a league and return instantly to the charge, returning to it frequently, but this is only when they are in great numbers, otherwise they flee, hoping to attack after dark. This can be stopped if one posts a strong guard. They will also seek to attack when their enemy is crossing a river or passing through a defile.

The prisoners they take are made into slaves and are sold to the merchants in Constantinople and other places in the Levant, which are sent to Cassa, or keep them for their personal service, such as guarding their herds or cultivating the ground in locations where they work. Among their prisoners are various Polish and French officers, including Lieutenant Colonel Nicolai and Captain la Croustade, who had unfortunately fallen into their hands. But the Poles treat them the same, except their children, which they take as servants after baptizing them and instructing them in the Christian Religion, and some *murza*, which they lock up and use to exchange for Polish lords who find themselves in Tartar hands. The others are treated as slaves and

---

⁴Translator: Two hundred years earlier this is the sort of wagon train used by Jan Hus, which he called a "wagenburg." However, the Hussites made it more formidable with trenches. The Boers used the same tactic and called it a "wagen laager." And the American pioneers moving across the western plains used to defend themselves against the Indians. I have decided that the Boer term is the most appropriate to describe this tactic and will place it in parenthesis after the original Polish term "tabor."

perpetually have irons on their legs, serving as beasts of burden carrying all sorts of burdens, lime, bricks, and other building material, firewood for the kitchen and chambers, cleaning houses, moving earth, and other similar works but they are always guarded. These miserable people have little opportunity to earn money, but what they might, they spend on food, as their ordinary food is bread and water unless they can catch a horse.

Pierre Chevalier

HISTORY
OF THE WAR OF THE COSSACKS AGAINST POLAND

Poland has often had to deal with powerful enemies. It has fought with the German Empire, with the Teutonic Knights since their establishment in Prussia, who were frequently supported with German assistance and with the Tartars, who make frequent incursions and sometimes cross Poland from one side to the other. Then, the Turks that came in 1621 to Khotyn, on the Dniester, with an army of 400,000 men. The Turks appeared about to engulf the kingdom. Later, the Poles were threatened by King Gustavus Adolphus, of Sweden, who was in Livonia with considerable forces. However, the Poles have always engaged these enemies, no matter how redoubtable, but none of these wars were more dangerous than the defection of the Cossacks, in 1648, which erupted almost at the moment when their king died. The rebels raised up almost all the people of Black Russia, who were stripped of their mortal and irreconcilable hatred that they had towards the Tartars, aligned with them and even implored the assistance of the Turks for the entire ruin and desolation of Poland.

Having joined their forces with those of the infidels, they made in less than four years, four great invasions into the kingdom, with armies of 200,000 or 300,000 formidable peasant infantry, hardened by work and the injuries of time, while battle hardened by the frequent raids of the Tartars into their lands. They found themselves supported by the Tartar cavalry which, without a doubt, would have been the best in the world, if it had been arranged and disciplined like that of the Christians.

Bogdan Khmelnytsky was the first spark of this blaze and the driver of this war. He was born a noble, son of the *podstarosta* of a Polish general, who was enrolled in the Cossack Militia as a simple soldier. He rose to the rank of captain and then was sent as a member from this militia to the Polish Diet, then to the Commissioner General and finally became a general. He was able to read; which was something very rare among these people.

King Władysław, bored with the apathy of the court, while he watched many other Christian kings and princes in action, meditated, in 1646, a war against the Perekop Tartars, which he wished to chase from the Crimea, found Khmelnytsky worthy of command of the Cossack Army. However, the King's plan was not seconded by the Christian princes, who were otherwise occupied, nor by the Venetians who were to send assistance, and the Polish Republic, having become disenchanted, was obliged to disband the troops that he had raised. A portion of those forces were raised using his wife's dowry. Thus Khmelnytsky found himself without employment, but he soon found other position.

On the limits of some of his property, an incident occurred where Czapliński, a lieutenant of Koniespolski, Grand Standard-bearer of the Crown apparently found reason to ill-treat Khmelnytsky's wife and strike his son with a stick during the course of a quarrel. Khmelnytsky soon found means to respond to this outrage, discovering that the Russians were unhappy with their being oppressed, as the peace had, instead of giving them repose, given the nobility the ability to hold them in servitude and oppression. Having carefully handled their discontent and being certain of his Cossacks, at the beginning of the year 1648 he withdrew towards Porouys or the Dnieper Islands to place himself out of range of attack by the Poles and to fortify himself.

Many have thought, with justification, that King Władysław, who again sought to take up his plan to send an expedition against the Tartars, undertook a secret communication with him and sought to stir up the Cossacks so as to oblige the Republic to give him an army to go against them. However, as he approached them, they were joined to his troops, which were, for the most part foreigners commanded by his confidants, who had no concern for the Republic's orders and followed this prince against the Tartars and the Turks, with whom it was later necessary to fight after having attacked the first. Be what it may, as Khmelnytsky saw that the letters that he had written in Poland to complain of the injuries received by the Cossacks and those that had been done to him in particular, even though full of submission and protestations of obedience, had had no effect; that to the contrary the Grand Hetman Potocki, prepared to march against him; as he mustered his troops, Khmelnytsky called on the Tartars for assistance. The Tartars were, at this time, wintering in the desert plains, seeking an opportunity to make their ordinary raids and brigandage in the Ukraine, where they were led by Tohaibeg, one of their chiefs, brave but mischievous, and frequently ignored to the Khan's orders.

The vast distance of the territory concealed knowledge of Khmelnytsky's plans from the Polish generals, giving him an advantage. Nevertheless, the Polish commanders believing they had firm information on his intentions, resolved to march on the Zaporovian Islands to crush this revolt in its crib. They hurried to the coast with some of the Polish army intended to guard the frontier, and, above all, the Cossack corps maintained in the service of the Republic, under the command of their commissioner Schomberg, Stephen Potocki, son of the general, and some other officers. A part of this Cossack Militia, which was embarked on the Dnieper arrived at Porouys, and immediately went over to Khmelnytsky, despite being newly registered with the Poles, which they thought void in favor of their compatriots. Khmelnytsky marched, notwithstanding, with this reinforcement before the other Cossacks who came overland arrived and quickly followed by marching out. In this last troop there were some companies of dragoons that rendered great services in this war against the Polish nobility.

The Poles, in order to spare themselves the expense of a German guard, which the great lords of this country were accustomed to have near their persons, had armed and uniformed some soldiers in the manner of the German dragoons, raising their courage by this change of conditions, as they were raised from slavery.

Khmelnytsky fortified by these defecting Cossacks, who totaled 4,000 men, had no difficulty in overcoming the remaining Polish troops, who numbered no more than 1,500 men. They defended themselves for a few days in the middle of their "tabor" [wagen laager], but having lost all their cannon and unable to resist the great number of their attackers, who surrounded them on all sides, they were all killed or taken prisoner by the Tartars. Sapieha was one of this group as well as Schomberg and Potocki, having been mortally wounded, could not be brought away and died on the field.

Khmelnytsky carefully handled this success and the acclaim that came from his first victory. He turned to face the rest of the Polish army, which still numbered 5,000 men. The Polish commanders, after having vainly waited for news of the march of the first troops, which they had detached towards the Dnieper, had finally received certain word of their defeat, the defection of the Cossacks, and the junction of the Tartars with the rebels. They believed it was necessary to retreat so as to save the rest of their forces, not thinking themselves capable of withstanding the rebels. However, the swiftness of the *bacmates* [the Tartar's horses], had not allowed them to move very far before the Tartars caught up with them and skirmishes began, in which some Tartars were taken prisoners. They were tortured and the Poles learned that their army numbered 40,000 and that there were 7,000 Cossacks, which were joined by the pashas of the colonies, which were coming from everywhere.

A Polish council of war considered if it was better to risk battle or to continue their retreat. However, it was not safe to remain any longer in that location as the Cossacks would soon prevent the receipt of food or forage, so the Poles chose to retreat in a wagon train. The Polish army had barely gone a half league when they entered a very thick forest whose heart was extremely swampy. Adding to their misery, the 1,800 Cossacks that had remained with them now abandoned them and joined their enemies. Finally, after having fought for four hours in the forest, as much with the bad roads as with the Cossacks, the *tabor* [*wagon laager*] was broken and driven in on all sides. Every Pole was killed, captured, or suffocated in the mud.

This disgrace, which occurred near Korsun, became even more painful in Poland because of the death of their King Władysław IV, at the same time at Merkinė, in Lithuania. He was 52 years old. No one doubted that this prince, whose valor joined to his many other great qualities, who was held in veneration by all his people and was redoubtable to his enemies, could have, by his authority and the respect for his name, dissipated the Cossack rebellion.

Khmelnytsky did not initially know of Władysław's death, and after his victory over the Polish army, he wrote a very submissive letter to this prince, in which he repeated everything that had occurred on the outrages of the governors, the rapine, the unjustifiable exactions made on the Jews, the seizing of the goods of several nobles, and of the domains of the King; he asked pardon of him for he had been obliged to guarantee himself, promising to send back the Tartars and to remain in obedience to His Majesty, provided that he would maintain him and his Cossacks and the privileges that had been accorded to them by the previous kings of Poland.

Sometime later he learned of the King's death by a letter sent to him by the Palatine of Braclaw, Adam Kisiel, carried by a Greek. This Palatine, who was also a schismatic Greek called on Khmelnytsky in the most soft and obliging terms to return to his duty, representing to him the ancient fidelity of the Zaporozhian Cossacks, in who, though very jealous of their liberty, they had always been very constant; that they lived in a Republic, where everyone, but most particularly the men of war, had always found sufficient liberty to attend to their interests and make complaints about any wrongs that they had suffered; that he [Khmelnytsky] was the only Senator of the Greek Religion, and in that capacity the protector of the churches and the rights of this religion, that he had always defended; that he was known by the holiness of this religion and by the honor of the Russian nation; that he should send the Tartars back to their homes and that he should return the Cossacks to their normal quarters, and when he deputized some of them to expose the injuries they had suffered, and he had personally suffered; that by their repetition, he offered his concerns and services to obtain the satisfaction that he might claim; that his rank in the Republic was real, that one could obtain no other resolution, be it peace or war, with his participation; but that he assured him that it was always easier to end these disorders by a peace than it was to maintain them by a continuation of a civil war; that their armies, which were currently occupied in their mutual ruin, could be better and more gloriously employed against the enemies of the Christians, which would serve them as a lesson to put to sleep the current troubles. He pointed out that the Tartars were divided by some discords, which would quickly turn to the use of arms, to settle their differences by this means, but that the first fire of their anger being past, they would reconcile themselves without arbiter or mediator; that this done that they would come together and not be held to this laudable process.

The bearer of this letter, having barely escaped the hands of the Tartars, arrived at Khmelnitsky's camp where he found considerable confusion. The Hetman, convening his soldiers, read this letter before them, and was the first to approve the advice of the Palatine of Braclaw. Having been supported by a majority of his soldiers, it was ordered that all acts of hostility would stop and they would wait for a response from the Polish Court; that the Tartars would be returned to the desert plains in the resolution that they would be ready at all times, and that the Palatine would be invited to come to them.

Khmelnitsky's moderation, in the state of his affairs, surprised everyone; however, he was not known to be deceptive. On one side it appeared that he had stopped the course of his victory to spare blood and to more easily obtain pardon; on the other he oriented his power towards the Poles so as to extort from them that which could not be given by simple submission.

Thus, he retired into the city of Bila Tserkvo, holding himself there while Kryvonis, the other Cossack chief, a vacuous man, but bold and horribly cruel, ravaged Russia and Podolia. Khmelnytsky appeared to disavow these ravages and promised to put Kryvonis and the five other rebel chiefs in Polish hands. However, this was only with the idea of amusing them and to give him the opportunity to capture the fortress at Bar.

Jeremi Michael, Prince of Wiśniowiec had gone to the extremity of Russia, beyond the Dnieper with some troops, where he joined the forces of Tyszkiewicz, Palatine of Kiev, and the Guards Regiment of the deceased King, commanded by Ossinski, Field Hetman of Lithuania[1], to oppose Kryvonis' raids, and stopped his progress for some time. Without this effort the Cossacks would have moved all the Russian population into the kingdom, which were no less than 100,000 men. Several other troops and the *arrière-ban*[2] of the nobility of the frontiers, having formed a new army, they marched on the Cossacks and rebelling peasants, after having made a second attempt to come to an accommodation with their leaders. This effort failed.

The Polish Republic, on this occasion, felt more strongly, on the occasion of the death of its king, that there was no one sufficiently authorized to command the so many qualified lords as were in this army. As a result disorder and dissention erupted among them, and the wisest among them, looking at the state of affairs, judged that it was absolutely necessary to avoid battle. Following this advice, it was resolved to withdraw in good order,

---

[1]This is the equivalent of a Lieutenant General or a French Maréchal de camp.
[2]Translator: The "ban" is a French military phrase signifying the convocation of vassals under the feudal system. Its etymology is mixed and uncertain. Under Charles VIII of France the ban and the arrière-ban meant an assembly of the ordinary militia. As the author of this work was French, it is certain that he is using this word in the French sense. In Polish this is called, "*Pospolite Ruszenie*"

within the shelter of a *tabor* [*wagen laager*] and to move to Starokostiantyniv. However, the orders were misunderstood and some troops received orders to decamp from the vicinity of Pilavcze and others did not await their orders and marched before their turn. Chaos resulted and the confusion greatly increased in the night, spreading a terror throughout the army that infected even the bravest, when they could not determine the subject of this flight and general consternation.

This could have assured a complete victory for Khmelnytsky, whose army was not subject to the same confusion. He knew so little of what occurred, however, that he mistook this flight as a Polish stratagem and could not give any faith in the reports of what happened. As a result, he did not order an aggressive pursuit of the fugitives and, instead, ordered a leisurely pursuit with much circumspection.

Eventually he realized the truth of what had happened, and moved aggressively against L'viv. It was a large city because of its commerce with the Levant and trade routes south. Khmelnytsky sought to strip it of food and the men appropriate for its defense.

The Poles had left Arcissewski in command of this city. He was a veteran officer who had a long history of service with foreign troops and commanded Dutch troops at Bresil. He held out for a promised relief force from Małopolska. The inhabitants of the city commanded by this officer, provided a sufficiently strong resistance for several days. However, when the castle was abandoned by those who defended it and taken by the besiegers, Arcissewski saw no point in holding out longer against the 300,000 man army that was before the city and starvation had begun to make itself felt. They bought off the Cossacks with a considerable sum.

The Cossacks having left L'viv and moved before Zamosc, a city recently fortified in the modern manner by Jan Zamoyski. Zamoyski was a general and Grand Chancellor of Poland, from the time of King Sigismund, the father of the last two kings. Zamosc had served as the only asylum of the Russian nobility that had been chased from their lands by the revolting peasants. However, a good part of those from the Palatinates of Belz and Sandomierz, found themselves in this fortress with the 1,500 men that Louis Weiher, Palatine of Pomerania, had led there from Prussia. All of the efforts made by the Cossacks and rebelling peasants for a month were useless. As a result, they withdrew into the depths of Russia.

It is not appropriate to pass silently over the assistance that the Polish Republic received from His Most Christian King [of France], even though the flame of civil war has begun to appear in France. He sent eight hundred recruits, raised at his expense by Colonel Khristofile Prziemski, who commanded a Polish regiment in his army of Flanders, to join the Polish army under the command of that colonel. They formed a good regiment.

Khmelnytsky had retired into winter quarters with his troops when some principal lords of the Republic came to speak to him on the part of the Republic about making peace. They only received proud responses, however, in light of all his victories in the previous campaign, which had made him more insolent than before, such that the deputies were lucky to obtain a truce for a few months.

Here and there began the preludes for a new war before the truce expired. The rebel troops provoked the Poles in various places, but they limited their aggression, having been beaten almost everywhere by Andrzej Firlej, Castellan of Belz and Stanisław Lanckoroński, Castellan of Kamianets, between whom the new King Jan Casimir immediately after his election, had divided the command of the armies. The Cossacks suffered, among others, notable checks at Zviohel, Ostropol, Bar, and other locations, which resulted in heavy losses among the rebels, in which the Poles took a rich booty.

Khmelnytsky impatiently awaited the arrival of spring, recalled the Tartars, who joined him with 100,000 men, and returned to the field to make a new raid into Poland. The Poles assembled to block his plan and their leaders, having deliberated at which post they should stop him, until the rest of the forces of the Kingdom joined them. Among the several opinions, it was finally decided to camp under the cannon of Kamianets. The importance of this fortress, which served as a barrier against the Turks, was such that it merited being preserved, over all considerations. This was the opinion of Firlej, and it prevailed, as he judged it appropriate to not move the army far from the frontier, which might expose the Kingdom to an invasion. He chose the city of Zbarazh, belonging to the Prince of Wiśniowiec, as a strong post appropriate for his plan and where he could receive the expected reinforcements. He had no more than 9,000 men, including the troops that some of the Polish lords had raised at their expenses. He had with him, among other officers, Lanckoroński, the Count of Ostrorog, the Grand Cupbearer of the Crown, who had been given to him for colleagues, Duke Demetrius, Jeremi Michael Wiśniowiecki and Alexandre Koniecpolski, Grand Ensign of the Crown, son of the deceased Grand General Koniecpolski.

General Firlej, anticipating that he would soon be surrounded by a nearly numberless army, quickly set about amassing food and repairing the old fortifications of the city and Zbarazh Castle, and covered his camp with a good entrenchment, flanked by forts and redoubts. He took particular care in assuring a type of pond which gave him an abundant source of water, such that it could not be diverted by the Cossacks.

General Firlej had barely completed his entrenchments when the army of the Cossacks and Tartars enveloped him from every side. They were so numerous that nothing that large had been seen since time of Attila and Tamerlane, and has not been seen since. The Tartar Khan was there in person and imagined himself engulfing the Kingdom of Poland as a prey that could not escape him and Khmelnytsky would not have failed to make him look infallible. The fact that this little handful of Polish soldiers, who were the only forces that appeared at that time for the defense of the frontier, he resolved not to starve them out but to carry their camp by assault. He thought to execute this easily as the strength of his army was such that there was no need to be sparing of his men.

Khmelnytsky gave the order to attack on 13 July 1649, and it was a furious assault. He was at the head of his troops, who did not know either the danger of the attack, nor the valor of the Poles. A great effort was made on the part of General Firlej to defend the castle, exposing himself at every part of the fighting. The assailants were covered by a nearby valley, such that some of them who had already forced the trench, were only chased out with difficulty. Firlej and Prince Wiśniowiecki defended themselves valiantly. The latter seeing his men beginning to waver, forbade them to fire on the Tartars, who he thought would bring words of friendship and peace to the generals. These troops, encouraged by this artifice, and persuaded that they only had to deal with the Cossacks, threw themselves so forcefully against them that after having cut down a great number of them, they pushed the rest of the Cossacks back, astonished by their desperate bravery, after having withstood 17 attacks that day.

The Cossacks renewed their attacks in the following days, but with even less success, even though they had their forces joined in stratagems. They had caused the Poles to believe that they were about to receive reinforcements from the Turks. To this end straw dummies, dressed in the Turkish manner, were placed on horses and led by a few men dressed in the same way. However, the Poles discovered this ruse by observing from their lunettes.

Khmelnytsky also sent them letters, in which he exhorted Firlej to come to an accommodation and solicited, by other letters, the German troops to desert. Finally, seeing that he could not win by ruse or direct assault, he resolved to attack the Polish entrenchments. He employed the huge number of rebel peasants in his army night and day digging approach trenches.

This new effort by the Cossacks embarrassed the Poles more than the earlier efforts. Seeing that they were coming and that they had only a small garrison in their front trenches, they dug more trenches near the city, into which they withdrew. Some of the ranking officers were of the opinion that they should abandon all exterior works and withdraw into the fortress, but this strategy was very dangerous and was not accepted. In addition the extremity in which they were reduced, they had almost no space to move and the garrison was beginning to lack food and forage. Their horses were dying daily and the stench made the camp difficult to occupy. A loaf of bread sold for 10 *poltoracs*.[3] A barrel of beer cost 50 florins. The soldiers were reduced to eating horses and dogs. Khmelnytsky, who constantly received deserters, knew the state of the besieged was becoming more and more difficult and now wished to grant them only the harshest conditions. The

---

[3]Translator: A poltorac was a Polish penny. There were 20 poltoracs to the florin.

Tartar Khan showed himself more humane, always asking that Wiśniowiecki and Koniespolski come to negotiate an end, and the Poles, never wishing that these lords place themselves in his hands, refused. The Polish generals sent messages to the King of Poland informing him of their desperate situation and asking prompt relief. However, almost all of these letters fell into the Cossacks' or Tartar's hands. The few that escaped had no response, as the returning messengers were either killed or taken.

Now and then a rare message got back to the city bringing news from His Polish Majesty that promised that relief would soon be there. In order to increase the faith of the garrison in these letters the King's Seal was removed from some letters and added to others. The Polish generals counseled patience to the besieged army with these letters as proof of help coming and the softness of their words.

Some of the principal Polish officers, who still had stocks of food, chose to eat the rotting dog and horse flesh in order to share the trials of their soldiers. Firlej, though broken by age and sickness, wished to do the same, but he was prevented from doing so by those around him. Wiśniowiecki and Koniespolski launched frequent sorties against the besiegers so as to deny them hope of a quick end, using the men who were still healthy and resolute. However, in addition to the lack of food, the Poles were running out of ammunition, which prevented them from firing as often as they had earlier. The Cossacks not rest for their continuous fire against the Polish camp and their innumerable assaults. They even attempted to cut off the Poles' water supply.

None of their efforts having succeeded so far, the Cossacks now attempted to set the city on fire, principally one of the gates, which greatly annoyed them. This gate was higher than the others and was manned by the best Polish shots, including Rittmeister Butler, who kept up a murderous fire on the Cossacks. The Jesuit Father Muchaweski, firing from the castle's gate, killed more than 200 Cossacks. A large troop of peasants, brandishing torches, moved against the gate with the objective of setting it on fire. Other groups approached other locations, but the garrison, who were advised of their plan, was prepared to frustrate their efforts, by standing firmly and leaving many dead.

Things were in this state when a letter, attached to an arrow, flew into the city. Its author, who is only known to be a knight, apologized that he was serving with the Cossacks, which he had been forced to because of the abuse he had suffered at the hands of a powerful lord, and the setbacks that the Poles had suffered in the previous year. He went on to declare that he had not lost his love for his homeland, which he had said to the garrison in three other letters that he had sent into the city. He informed them that the King of Poland was coming to their relief and that he was already at Zborov. The Cossacks knew this and would surely redouble their efforts, but that the garrison must be prepared to redouble their defensive efforts.

Most of the garrison gave the letter no credence, believing it to be a trick, but it was, in fact, true. The King of Poland had advanced to Zboriv to rescue the besieged troops, after having surmounted all the obstacles that had delayed their march. It is true that his army did not appear, to the most intelligent, sufficient to deal with the incredible multitude of the Cossack Army, which it was about to encounter, but was only a token force. It consisted of only 15,000 regulars and 5,000 others raised by some lords in their domains. The rest of the nobility was unable to come, either being called too late or they disobeyed the calls of the King, who pressed them for a long time.

Khmelnytsky and the Khan having known of the march of the King of Poland, divided their forces and left 40,000 Tartars with 200,000 Cossacks and peasants around Zbarazh, then marched on Zboriv with around 60,000 Tartars and 80,000 Cossacks. They concealed their march so well from the King that he received no news of their movement, be it that he had not sent forward patrols to observe the Cossacks or more likely because the local peasants favored the Cossacks.

As a result the Cossacks and Tartars arrived before the royal camp without being observed, because of the woods and thick fog, as well as the negligence of the Poles. Khmelnytsky actually entered into the city of Zboriv and observed the Polish army at leisure.

The exit from Zboriv was a great defile formed by levies and bridges over the swamps close to it, and as the Polish army began to clear that defile and move into the open field the Cossacks and Tartars suddenly fell on them. The battle began by the attack on some Polish baggage. The Tartars then took the Royal Polish troops in the rear, having crossed a stream, which the peasants had made crossable by breaking a levy. The nobility of Premyśl and the cavalry of the Duke of Ostrog sustained the first shock, but could not resist the great number of the Tartars before them. Several of the nobility remained there with all their baggage. Stanislaw Witkowski and Leon Sapieha, Vice Chancellor of Lithuania, came to their support, driving back the Tartars. However, the Tartars returned with greater impetuosity against the Vice Chancellor's troops, who would have succumbed after a six hour battle in which they charged three times, if Jerzy Ossoliński, the Castelan of Sandomierz, and Bydgoszcz, Starosta of Stabnitz, had not made a diversion to distract the infidels. Ossoliński remained there with several units of the Palatinate of Russia. As all this was occurring on the flanks and rear of the Polish army, Khmelnytsky attacked it frontally with his Cossacks and part of the Tartars. The King, who at the first sound of their arrival had arranged his troops in battle, had given the command of the right wing to Grand Chancellor Ossoliński. This wing was formed from the King's cavalry, which included troops from the Palatines of Podolia, Enhoff, Starosta of Sokal and Beltz, and other regiments. He left to Jerzy Lubormirski, Starosta of Cracow, and to Duke Korecki, command of the left wing, where, among others, were their cavalry regiments and several companies of volunteers.

The battle [formation] consisted of the infantry and where the King had taken his post. It was commanded by General Major Hubald, originally of Misnie, who was a veteran of the wars in Germany, and had been commandant of the Gdansk Militia, and by Sir Władysław Zasławski, Governor of Cracow. These two men had their respective regiments with them.

The Tartars remained away from the Poles giving the appearance that they only wished to observe to fighting. Then, they suddenly charged forward according to their typical manner of fighting. However, they were received roughly by the Poles. The Tartars found the infantry armed with pikes in a formation that could not be overwhelmed, so they swept to the left, passing that wing. Korecki, who was in the front rank, had his horse killed under him and he decided to remain there. Ruzowski was wounded by an arrow, which pierced his cheeks. He left the arrow in his cheek as he went to the King to inform him of the danger to his left wing. His Polish Majesty, forgetting his dignity and his person, immediately rode to the left wing to bolster their morale by his presence and by his exhortations to their courage. All those who had turned to flee returned to the fight after he told them, that having no other officers to send, he had come himself. The King would have pushed into the melee himself if his escorts had not restrained him. The presence of the King exposing himself raised the courage of his troops, which the terrible multitude of Tartars and Cossacks had so shaken.

Some Tartars made headway of one flank, but they were quickly pushed back by the discharges of the Polish cannons and two companies of infantry commanded by Captain Ghiza, of the King's Guard Regiment. The Cossacks achieved no success against the Polish army and night ended the battle. All the night was spent in conferences and the issuing of orders to receive the attack expected to come in the morning. The Poles also dug some entrenchments to protect themselves and the baggage took up a stronger position. Meanwhile the King deliberated with his principal lords and the army's officers when a rumor spread through the camp that the King intended to withdraw that night with most of the army.

The extreme peril in which the Poles were reduced made a retreat plausible, so shortly great consternation appeared, similar to that of Pilaucze. The King, who had gone to bed, was awakened, mounted his horse, and rode through the camp assuring the men that no such order had been or would be issued, that he had never considered such an order, but that it was necessary to remain firm before the enemy, flattering them with the hope of a favorable success of the battle, which would surely start that morning. Among the suggestions from the council of war on the present situation, that to attempt to detach Khmelnytsky from the Khan was the most supported. The Khan was sent a letter, carried by a Tartar prisoner, reminding him of the many favors given him by the deceased King Władysław, who had taken him prisoner, treated him favorably and then released him, as well as raising him to his present dignity. It went on to say that after having done this, he was surprised that he had joined the rebels and the serfs, but that he should not promise him great advantages from such an unjust association. God cannot favor such plans. However, His Majesty having found it appropriate to remember the obligation he had to the deceased king, his brother, he would offer him his friendship [if he broke his alliance with the rebels].[4] No response was forthcoming and the next morning the whole army of the Cossacks and Tartars appeared in battle formation, some turning towards the city of Zborov and the others falling on the baggage.

Meanwhile, 400 light horse occupied the Cossacks with skirmishes for some time; then having been supported by a larger number of men, pushed the Cossacks away from the city and the servants,[5] who were with the baggage train assisted in repulsing the Tartars.

The Cossacks then divided into three corps and attacked the Royal camp in three areas, after first seizing a church, which commanded a view of the camp. The Poles then directed the fire of a battery against this position, which obliged the Cossacks to withdraw. The Poles made themselves masters of the church, while one of their most determined soldiers placed a flag in the entrenchment. A large body of royal troops ran up and bravely defended this position, forcing the Cossacks to abandon their attack and the battle. The retainers came out to pursue them and the courage that they showed on this occasion

---

[4] Translator: There is a fragment of a sentence relating to the rebel alliance, but with a word that I was unable to decipher. Since it was the intent of this letter to pull Khmelnytsky away from the rebel army, it seemed logical that the last bit of this letter would be directed to that end.

[5] In addition to regular troops, the retinue of nobles, teamsters and the militar would sometimes be armed during the battle to act as irregular soldiers.

caused some to suggest that they be mounted and distributed among the other forces to augment their numbers and with this reinforcement drawn from the army itself, risk a battle. However, the others, for the most part, opposed risking anything, since if they were defeated they would be reduced to an extreme situation. The various and uncertain of opinions in the Polish leadership, would not allow them to come of a decision on the next course of action. However, Providence intervened. The Tartar Khan, had been promised certain victory in these attacks against the Polish army, was starting to lose heart for continuing the campaign, began to appear inclined for a settlement. Thus, he made a very civil response to the King's earlier letter by which he recognized his debt to the Royal House and expressed that if His Majesty, after his election, had sought him out, he would have been friendlier to his interests than those of the Cossacks. However, he had been neglected. He said that if an occasion should present itself to renew his old alliance with the King, he would lay down his arms, and help return the Cossacks to their duty, provided that the old treaties were renewed. He finally stated that if His Majesty desired to name a location where negotiations might be held and one could find his Chancellor there, the Khan would send his Vizier there. The letter from the Khan was accompanied by another from Khmelnytsky that was very respectful, by which, he assured the King of his fidelity and his future services.

The Polish King agreed to a conference and a place was chosen between the two armies. The Vizier was the first to arrive and when the First Chancellor Ossoliński arrived, the Vizier requested that the Polish King pay the pension or pay [tribute] that the Polish Republic had been accustomed to give to the Khan for his service, which he would render to Poland and that the deceased King

Władysław had refused to pay. He asked that first they satisfy the Zaporozhian Cossacks and that the Tartars be compensated for this expedition and the blood that they had poured out; that they be given permission to raid and pillage the land in complete liberty during their return.

There was, during this discussion, a suspension of arms which was constantly interrupted by some hostilities. The next day, which was 17 August, the plenipotentiaries returned to the same location. Both of them were accompanied by two others, the Chancellor of the Commonwealth had with him the Palatine of Kiev and the Vice Chancellor of Lithuania. The Vizier had Sieserkaz with him and Suliman Aga. Khmelnytsky added to the negotiations a request for amnesty for himself, the Cossacks, and the peasants who had revolted; that they be assured their liberty, and their Greek Orthodox Religion. Finally, after some discussions and negotiations, a peace treaty was negotiated with the Tartars and the Cossacks under the following conditions:

1.) *There shall be peace and fraternal friendship in the future between Jean Casimir King of Poland and his successors and Islam Giray, Khan of the Tartars and those of the House of Giray.*
2.) *That the King shall liberally pay the pension or ordinary pay [tribute] to the Tartars, in sending a request to Kamianets by express deputy.*
3.) *That the Khan would be required to join the King with all his troops against whatever enemy, when called upon to do so.*
4.) *The Khan guaranteed the frontiers of Poland from the raids and brigandage of his subjects.*
5.) *That the rest of his troops remaining before Zbarazh would decamp and allow the Polish troops that were there*

to freely depart, and go to whatever place His Polish Majesty might designate.

6.) That the Khan would withdraw, without delay from the lands of said Majesty, all his troops and any Turks that might be with them.

7.) That the King would, in consideration to the Khan, accord a general pardon to Khmelnytsky and his army, and re-establish the Cossack Army in its old form, number, and liberty.

8.) Beyond these conditions, [the King of Poland] promised 300,000 florins to the Khan, who would then receive 100,000.

The advantages accorded to Khmelnytsky were very substantial. They were:

1.) A general amnesty to all the Cossacks and rebel peasants and that all that had passed would be treated as if it had not happened.

2.) That Khmelnytsky, their general, would request pardon of His Majesty on his knees and prostrated.

3.) That Khmelnytsky would continue as general of said Cossacks, whose number would be augmented to 40,000, who would depend only on the King, after he shall have issued an act recognizing him as a Polish Gentleman with regard to the Republic.

4.) That His Polish Majesty would have a list of the names and residences of said 40,000 Cossacks, so that in case Khmelnytsky should die, they shall be commanded by one of their leaders, who were a member of the Greek Orthodox Religion.

5.) That the army besieged at Zbarazh should be set at liberty.

6.) That the Greek Orthodox Religion should be exercised by anyone in the Kingdom, including Cracow, and that its union with the Roman Church should end.[6]

7.)   That the Palatinate of Kiev shall always be given to a Greek [Orthodox?] lord.

8.)   That the Metropolitan of the Greek Orthodox Religion shall always be in the Senate among the Bishops and shall occupy the ninth place.

9.)   That the Cossacks shall have permission to make brandy for their own use, but not for sale.

10.) That they shall be furnished cloth for clothing themselves and each shall receive 10 florins to arm themselves.

11.) That the nobles returned to their domains shall not seek to trouble their subjects for compensation for any losses that they had suffered.

12.) That said nobles, be they Catholic or Greek, who have remained loyal to the General of the Cossacks, will not be disturbed but forgiven for all that has occurred in these last wars.

In execution of this treaty Khmelnytsky went before the King and on his knees, tears in his eyes, made a great speech to express to the King his desire to receive the King's approval for the considerable service rendered to His Majesty and to the Republic, in which so much blood had been spilled; but that since Destiny had disposed otherwise, he came to implore his clemency and request in all humility a pardon for all past errors, protesting to repair them by his future conduct. The King responded to him, through the Vice Chancellor of Lithuania, that he sought the repentance of his subjects over their chastisement; that he forgave him with a good heart the past on the basis that he would wipe clean by his zeal and his fidelity towards the Fatherland, the crime that he had committed.

---

[6]This is a reference to the "Uniates" who worshiped in the Orthodox way, but recognized Papal authority

After the agreement was made Khmelnytsky and the Khan withdrew their troops and the King, too happy to have escaped from a military disaster so cheaply, marched on Gliniani with the Polish army. He then moved on L'viv. The troops entrenched at Zbarazh, reduced to the extremity as mentioned earlier, had maintained themselves there with rage and despair, more than with any hope of relief.

The inhabitants of this city could no longer suffer the starvation imposed on them by the siege and were at the point of burning the city or surrendering to the Cossacks. However, the vigilance of the Poles had prevented the execution of this tragic design. The inhabitants then asked that they be allowed to leave the city, but it was only granted to their women and children. As they could not hide their departure, they would first fall into the hands of the Cossack soldiers, who would abuse them as they wished, and finally, into the hands of the Tartars, who would take this unfortunate troop captive. Some servants of the Polish army were joined to this group.

On 21 August, the Cossacks gave the besieged the first news of the Peace of Zboriv, which some believed, but the others did not, thinking that they had not been included in the peace treaty. They were confirmed in this opinion by a trumpeter, who had the temerity to broadcast the same thing by a cry which he made in his movement. This would have cost him his life if one of the generals had not interceded. A letter from Khmelnytsky arrived shortly thereafter, by which he assured the besieged of their deliverance, by paying a sum to the Tartars. The generals did not wish to accept this condition for their liberty and said in a word that since Khmelnytsky was obliged to retire his troops, he would be satisfied, and for the Tartars, they could remain in their posts if they wished. Finally a more faithful and more joyous message arrived, carried by

Colonel Minor from the King to assure them of their liberty without any condition. As the Palatine of Sandomierz was vacant with the death of the Prince Zasławski, the King of Poland, in recognition of the services of General Firlej, he was given that position. Prince Wiśniowiecki was also given the Starosta of Pezemyl; the Duke of Ostrog that of Nessewitz; the Landskoronski that of Stobnik and of the Palatinate of Braclaw.

The other compensations given out were not as grand as these, but all the lords who had fought in its defense received wonderful compensations for the two months that they had been besieged and continuously attacked in Zbarazh.

God declared himself no less in favor of the Poles in Lithuania, than he had in Russia, where he came to pull, so to say, by the hand, their two armies from danger where according to all appearances, they should have perished.

The rebellion of the Cossacks and the Russian peasants had spread, from the beginning of the war, into Lithuania as a matter of course, as the people of this province were very similar, in their customs and religion, to the Russians.

The Cossacks had entered it from two directions, making some raids into Polesia, which is a country covered with woods and great swamps, that bordered with the Palatines of Kiev and Volhynia. It was seized by a treason that favored their attack on the cities of Starodub and Homel. Colonels Patz and Volouitz, then Prince Janusz Radziwiłł, Starosta of Samogitia and Field Hetman of Lithuania, opposed their plans as best as they could with the nobility of Orsa, the garrison of Beszowa, and some other troops they gathered. However, this relief from the Republic came too late and Prince Radziwiłł went the Diet for the new King's election, the rebels profited from his absence to attack Sluczk, a city belong to Prince Bogusław Radziwiłł Master of the Stables of Lithuania.

Sosnowski, who was governor, defended himself bravely against them and Horsch, Governor of Orsa, defeated 1,500 men at Czeresko. He then chased them before Beszowa. Mirski, the General Major of the Army of Lithuania, retook the city of Prinzko from them, a large city which was the seat of the Greek Bishop. The rebels had taken this city because of the treason of the inhabitants. Hladki, one of the principal Cossack officers, who was positioned in the city to defend it, was killed. As this place was one of their principal bases, it was sacked and burned to serve as an example.

By this time Prince Radziwiłł returned from the election of the King of Poland. Though the season was inappropriate for war, the simple rumor of his return, forced the surrender of the cities of Turov and Grodek, he encamped before the city of Mozyr, which was stubbornly defended for several days until it was taken by storm by Ganskowski, lieutenant colonel of the Radziwiłł Regiment. Michnenko, one of the rebel chiefs, was captured and beheaded by the executioner. His head was then placed on a tower of the castle.

From there he marched with his troops towards the Berezina River, where he attacked Bobroisko, whose inhabitants obtained grace from him on the condition that they hand over their arms and the authors of this upraising, or who had been in league with the Cossacks. Those among them who learned of this and were to be handed over retired into a wooden tower, which they set on fire, preferring a voluntary death to that with which they were threatened by the victor. Podubitz, who commanded them, received punishment appropriate for their rebellion as well as othrs.

The winter and the truce having stopped the war in both Lithuania and Poland for several months, Khmelnytsky retired into the Kingdom in the spring and sent Ilja Holota into that province to resume the war with 10,000 men, who was joined by many rebels. This Cossack general sought to surprise a part of the Lithuanian army that was in winter quarters at Zahal, on the Pripecz River, but Radziwiłł's troops were quickly assembled and put him to flight. The rebels were driven into a swamp where Holota died with his army. Khmelnytsky replaced him with Stephan Podobaylo, giving him orders to move between the Dnieper and the Zula River, which he did and set fire to Loiovogorod, fearing that this place would serve as a retreat for the Lithuanians. However, Gozieuski, having been detached with some troops to oppose his plans, after having crossed the Dniester, captured a post capable of greatly incommoding him. Khmelnytsky sent another 30,000 men into Lithuania, under the command of a Polish gentleman named Krychevsky.

Krychevsky, having otherwise procured his liberty from Khmelnytsky, received the same grace after the defeat of the Polish army at Korsun, the previous year. The favorable treatment that he received brought him into Khmelnytsky's service.

After moving into Lithuania, and crossing the Pripet, he thought to besiege Rzeczicza, an advantageously situated city, but instead he marched on Prince Radziwiłł camp, imagining, based on the information given him that Radziwiłł had detached some regiments and would be an easy target. He arrived at a point very close to Radziwiłł's camp after a silent march. However Chodorkovitz came out at the first rumor of his arrival with some cavalry, supported by 400 infantry commanded by Podlek and Juskievitz, and opposed the initial Cossacks attacks. While the Poles stopped the Cossacks with various charges, the rest of their troops slowly arranged themselves into battle formation. Gonzievski and Nievarovitz then pushed forward their hussars[7] against the Cossack left wing and into a wood near it. Initially they executed a heavy fire, knocking down some Cossacks that had moved too far forward. However, they were later constrained to move into the wood, where they were no longer able fight effectively. At the same time, some Polish squadrons, whose enthusiasm had carried them too far forward, were enveloped by the Cossacks and would have been torn to pieces if Komorowski with 1,000 men, who Prince Radziwiłł had detached before the battle, to reconnoiter the Cossack position, take some prisoners and gather news, had not arrived to save them. The leader who commanded the Cossack right wing saw these reinforcements arrive. He was not entrenched and saw this as a threat. Concerned that this force was being followed by a larger force and he was about to be ambushed, he retired into the woods.

In the meantime, Cossack General Pobodailo, who had come to the relief of Krychevsky with 12,000 men, brought them across the Dnieper in boats. It is certain that if he had arrived a bit sooner, and before the troops of the other had withdrawn, the Lithuanian army would have found itself in an extreme danger.

Barely half of Pobodailo's troops had crossed and begun to entrench themselves, however, when Prince Radziwiłł quickly attacked on them. After firing a ragged volley the Cossacks were put to rout and pushed into the river, such that 4,000 of them were killed or drowned. The reserve of 3,000 to 4,000 saved itself by swimming. Colonels Tisenhausen, Nold, and Fectman launched their Germans on the rest of Pobodailo's troops, which moved to join

[7] A footnote indicates that these were "lancers", which suggests that they were the famous Polish winged hussars.

Krychevsky with their tabor [wagen laager]. This general came out of the woods into which he had retired and was immediately struck by the Polish hussars, which obliged him to entrench himself behind an abattis of fallen trees. Learning the next night, by spies, that Prince Radziwiłł was preparing a new attack for the next day, he withdrew quickly, abandoning his heavy baggage. Krychevsky was wounded several times and abandoned in the road where he fell into Lithuanian hands. He died shortly later in their camp. Notwithstanding this check, the war re-ignited more strongly and 60,000 Cossacks crossed the Pripyat at Babica to launch a new invasion of Lithuania and re-establish their party. When the peace of Zboriv was concluded these Cossacks were recalled from Lithuania and Poland.

THE SECOND COSSACK WAR
1650

The King of Poland had returned to Warsaw to the acclamations of his people, who could not sufficiently express their joy and their gratitude for what he had done to conserve the Kingdom. He now turned to arrange, in the Sejm, all that he tried to do at the end of the year to assure the peace concluded with the Tartars and the Cossacks. The result of this Sejm, which finished on 12 January 1650, was that the Polish soldiers would be rewarded; that the army that had been besieged in Zbarazh, in consideration for its great services, would receive three extraordinary payments; that the Crown would continually maintain an army of 12,000 men for the protection of the frontier; that the articles of the treaty signed by Poland and the Cossacks and Tartars at Zboriv would be confirmed; that three new Cossack regiments should be admitted to the public charge; that to provide for all the great expenses a new tax would be imposed on all of Poland and Lithuania; and that it would be granted to His Majesty a new right, on all the merchandise, as a result of his exploits in the last campaign. It was also found appropriate to establish a senator at Kiev to closely oversee the actions of the Cossacks and to resolve any differences that might arise in the execution of the treaty. Adam Kisiel was named by the King to the Palatinate of this city. He was the most appropriate for the dignity of this commission and for the enrolling of the 40,000 men that were to form the Cossack Army, according to the last peace, and to give them the appropriate regulations.

Khmelnytsky maintained this peace for nearly a year and gave every appearance of maintaining good intentions, but he learned that the Poles that had forced him into a bad situation with the execution of this agreement, were imposing excessive conditions on him, were unrepentant, and sought the means to evade the conditions of the peace. Being the situation he looked to create other strong alliances to assure his position and enjoy the terms granted him.

In this vein, he sought the support of the Porte [Ottoman Empire] and of the Grand Duke of Moscow, but he especially favored the former, which he hoped would place him in formidable position. He also sought out the Hospodar or Prince of Moldavia, but in another fashion, corresponding with him in secret. He began by giving false impressions of the Prince to the Ministers of the Great Lord [Sultan], in the belief that he was secretly their enemy and showed him as the confidential friend of the Poles, who he provided their plans as well as those of the Tartars. The Ottoman Ministers, having assured Khmelnytsky of the protection of the Great Lord, and that he would be invested in Russia with an Imperial Ottoman fief, after having received from him his assurances of dependency and fidelity to his service, they permitted him to carry-out his plans against the Prince of Moldavia. He executed them with much cleverness and dissimulation, using the Tartars, to whom he joined 4,000 Cossacks. To better cover this game, the Khan had by his deputies thanked Khmelnytsky for the support that he had sent him against the Circassians, asking him for more troops to enter into Moscow in order to avenge himself of some injuries that he had suffered from the Grand Duke. This was so well done that the neighboring princes thought that the Tartars were going to make war in Moscow and the Hospodar, who was among that number, remained oblivious, in a profound peace, only to find himself invaded by a massive Tartar army and these 4,000 Cossack auxiliaries.

The Tartar invasion was so quick that the Hospodar of Moldovia was barely able to escape into the woods near his capital, Iaşi, in the depth of which he entrenched himself and his family behind an abattis of cut trees. He also gathered some men in haste, but he eventually agreed was to give the Tartars 20,000 ducats and promise his daughter's hand in marriage to Khmelnytsky's son Timothy. In addition, he accepted various other harsh conditions that were imposed on him.

The peace in the Ukraine, however, was quickly violated by the Cossacks, their vast army pushing its lines forward into Poland, supported by the peasants who did not wish to return to their gentlemen[1] , finally coming back to their lands. To which the nobility was mistreated and many of them massacred. Because of these actions and the operation on Moldavia, Generalissimo (Grand Hetman) Potocki, who had recently returned from Tartar captivity, moved the Polish army to Kamianets.

Khmelnytsky was very alarmed by Potocki's march. When he received first notice of this movement he had some deputies and nobles with him, who had come to complain about the peasant's rebellion and of their refusal to recognize their obligations to the nobles. He commanded, therefore, that all these deputies be drowned the next night. These orders were given while he was in his cups and those who were charged with this were on the point of executing it when Khmelnytsky woke up, after having dressed, and was warned by his wife of what was about to happen and he revoked the order. He subsequently sent Krawczenski, one of his officers, to General Potocki,

---

[1]Translator: The author uses the term "gentlemen" (pan) to mean a level of nobility other than the great lords; i.e. the dukes, princes, and counts.

to inform him of his astonishment at the approach of Polish troops at a time when the Republic was at peace with everyone, and that he, Khmelnytsky, had at his disposal a very powerful army of Cossacks intended for the defense of the frontier. General Potocki responded to this deputy about the daily violations of the treaty in the form of the bad treatment of the nobility by their subjects and by the war that Khmelnytsky had undertaken against the Prince of Moldavia; that in his capacity as General (Grand Hetman) of the Republic, he had to warn him about this. He added that he could not leave his post, which he had taken by command of the King, without the express command of His Majesty. This response did not please Khmelnytsky's deputy, but the General continued saying that His Majesty was very dissatisfied and suspicious because of his threats of war. However, no rupture occurred, either by the Polish army or by Grand Hetman Potocki, whose merit he admired and whose courage he feared, as Potocki attempted to dissuade him from creating his own principality, suggesting he did not have the resources to hatch this ambitious plot, and that he was against Khmelnytsky's expedition to Moldavia to find a new ally, even if by force.

The nobility was very badly led in the Ukraine, however, acting as if they were still at war. They were so badly led that many, including most of the lords who had great domains, were obliged to withdraw daily as they drew almost no revenues from their domains. Among them was the Prince of Wiśniowiec. The continual complaints that they made to the King caused him to write to Khmelnytsky. He reproached him for the war which he had undertaken without his order against the Hospodar of Moldavia and the outrages that the nobles were receiving. He enjoined him to withdraw the Zaporozhian Army to its quarters and to chastise the peasants that had armed themselves against their lords. He received this letter with great respect, but he proceeded with great slowness in executing what the King desired of him. To the contrary he worked at the same time to align himself more strongly with the Turks and the Grand Duke of Moscow. He aggressively sought an alliance that would provide him with more security and more so with the Grand Duke because of their common religion. However, the Grand Duke had earlier sought to profit from this support, did not approve of it.

The great successes enjoyed by Khmelnytsky over the Poles, who the Grand Duke was persuaded were entirely crushed and beaten, had gotten him into a drunken argument with Khmelnytsky, as he hoped to obtain from him in the bad state of their affairs, the revocation of the treaty that the Muscovites had been obliged to make with the deceased King Władysław at Smolensk, where he disarmed and captured all of the Muscovite army that garrisoned that fortress. The Grand Duke requested compensation for the affront that he had received from several Polish lords, among others Prince Wiśniowiecki and Koniespolski, who had not addressed him with all his titles, but had also written him, in terms most injurious to the reputation of the Muscovite nation. This compensation was to cede to him the city of Smolensk with its dependencies and pay him a sum of 180,000 ducats. The King of Poland sent a gentleman named Barlinski to the Grand Duke to discuss with him the insolent requests of his ambassador, who he was holding. This envoy reported that he believed the Muscovite was more inclined to observe the ancient treaties with Poland rather than break them. In effect, as delighted as he was to see the growth of the Greek Religion, he did not look with pleasure on the progress made by Khmelnytsky, out of fear that the revolt of the Cossacks and the peasants would spread into his lands, where some sparks of the fire that had embraced Poland had already fallen.

The continual relations between Khmelnytsky and the Turks, of which the King of Poland was advised by the princes neighboring his enemies, and his insolent misconduct towards the Republic, obliged the King of Poland to convoke the General Diet of the Kingdom at the end of the year 1650, in which he spoke of the insupportable conduct of Khmelnytsky, the misunderstandings of Khmelnytsky towards him and the Republic, the outrages suffered by several gentlemen despoiled of their goods and who had not yet re-established themselves, that he was attempting to expand his army with those of the Tartars and even the Turks, that he could in a moment assemble an army of more than 80,000 men, every Cossack enlisted, whose number, by the last treaty had risen to 40,000 claiming each to have a mounted servant, another on foot, in addition to a servant for work; that their plan was completely throw off the yoke of the Republic and to form a separate state, under the protection of the Great Lord [Sultan of the Ottoman Empire]; that they were capable of undertaking any enterprise, if they did not stop at the earliest possible moment their pernicious designs. There were some men in this assembly who had suffered greatly in the last war and who preferred peace, in whatever form, alleging that the forces of the Kingdom were greatly diminished, while those of the Cossacks remained very powerful by themselves, let alone without the assistance of the Ottomans, who protected them; that it was better to live under the Treaty of Zboriv. Others, however, who were in the majority, looked both at the future and the past, recognized that there were two options: one to ruin the Cossacks, or the other a miserable death for the Kingdom. They argued that the King had no authority over them and to do nothing would produce terrible results if they gave him the time to grow and strengthen his forces. They formed a plan of action. They interpreted the treaty in a manner and in a sense that pleased them. They argued that the Republic still had considerable forces, provided they could be used sparingly and that in their current state they were capable of stopping this new and growing power that threatened the Republic, when it was raised and fortified over time; that the King was brave, vigorous, active, and that he had, with small armies, gained great successes over his enemies, and that the Republic was capable of great efforts. However, new demands sent by the Cossacks caused the deputies of the Diet to return and they resolved unanimously for war against the Cossacks. These demands were that following one of the articles of the Peace of Zboriv, the union with the Greeks and the Roman Catholics be abolished; that Khmelnytsky remain sovereign beyond the Dnieper, that no other Polish lord or gentleman should have, in the future, power over the peasants of this province; that if the gentlemen wished to remain there, they would be obliged to work like the peasants; that the nine bishops swear, in the open Senate, to observe all the foregoing, and that one give as hostages to Khmelnytsky four palatines of his choice. In return for this he promised the King of Poland a million florins every year. Subsequently they reduced all these demands to four, saying that if they were put in possession of a land where they could live without having any communication with the Poles; that His Majesty and twelve of the principal lords of the Kingdom took an oath to always obey the Peace of Zboriv; that three of these senators would remain close to Khmelnytsky and that there would no longer be a union between the Roman Catholic and Greek Orthodox Churches [2]. However, even these limited demands were found exorbitant and no one thought

---

[2] The "Uniates" followed the eastern rite, but recognized Rome's authority

that they could be assured of the faith of a man who did not content himself with what the King and Republic had undertaken by their confirmation of the Treaty of Zboriv by the previous Diet.

The Diet had no thought other than war. They resolved to undertake a levy of 50,000 paid soldiers and the convocation of the *arrière-ban*, using the *arrière-ban* as a reserve to be used at the last extremity, and that it was better to augment the number of paid soldiers. It was also proposed to begin the war before the arrival of spring in order to deny the Cossacks time to make their preparations and to be able to engage them before the thaw of the swamps and rivers, which ordinarily covered their marches and their encampments. In addition it would be very difficult for them to gain support from the Turks and the Tartars during the winter. The Turks were not accustomed to the rigors of the cold and the Tartars would not be able to find forage for their horses. However, this project could not be fully executed, as the troops raised by the Diet could not be mobilized by that time. The King only detached Maréchal de camp (Crown Field Hetman) Kalinowski to cover the frontier and protect it from any incursions of the Cossacks. In the case that they preferred peace to war, it was agreed one last time to offer the Cossacks the terms of the Treaty of Zboriv. They were, however, quickly made aware of Khmelnytsky's intentions, which were contrary to peace, by the hostilities that began on the frontier. Nieczay, one of his general majors, with 3,000 men under his command, put all the land to fire and blood and massacred the Deputies of the Palatine of Braclaw in the presence of the Turkish envoy. The Cossacks were pursued by the troops of this Palatine and those of Kalinowski into the city of Krasne, where part were torn to pieces when they attempted to leave after abandoning the castle that they could no longer defend. Among others, a noble named Baibuza killed Nieczay with his hand, forcing the rest into some villages which were sacked and reduced to cinders. Another Cossack general named Bohun replaced Nieczay, attacked Kalinowski, capturing the city of Vinnytsia on the Bug, but the Poles, having crossed this river with much difficulty, and took the castle by assault, in which they killed a number of their enemies. The Cossacks were reinforced by one of their colonels named Gluki, They then chased out the Poles and re-entered the fortress. Finally, after Bohun, was reinforced by the Cossack regiments of Czherin, Prziluka, Lubiecz, and Braclaw, each of 2,000 men, Kalinowski was obliged to abandon the village, leaving a guard of some infantry with their servants and the baggage of his army.

Kalinowski then arranged his army in battle formation on the neighboring field, but spread the Winicza garrison throughout their ranks. They abandoned the city after pillaging the Polish baggage. The Cossacks then swarmed the Polish troops from all sides and drove them in disorder under the cannon of Bar, inflicting on them the loss of 4,500 infantry and all their artillery.

This check obliged the King of Poland, who had gone on a pilgrimage to Zurowitz, a place of devotion in Lithuania, to quickly move on the frontier where Grand General (Grand Hetman) Potoski was assembling troops in the vicinity of Sokal. While in Lublin he learned of the Cossack penetration into Podolia and the confederation formed between Khmelnytsky and the Grand Seigneur [Sultan] as well as receiving other news from the Emperor's [Holy Roman Empire] ambassador to the Porte. As a result he issued the last convocation of the arrière-ban.

Kalinowski, retired from Bar to Kamianets, received orders to move diligently towards the main army, after having left a sufficient garrison for the city of Kamianets.

This fortress was very important to Poland, as well as to all Christianity.

Kalinovski was followed, in his march, by 18,000 Cossacks and 2,000 Tartars. The rest of their troops, estimated to be more than 70,000 men, resolved to attack Kamianets, though without the orders or knowledge of their general. After having taken Panofcze Castle, near it by ruse, they took considerable booty, then launched multiple assaults against this fortress, which were in vain, always being pushed back with such heavy losses the besiegers were close to tearing their leaders to pieces for having sent them on such a dangerous mission. Khmelnytsky, who learned of this, sent them orders to decamp.

The Cossacks who relentlessly pursued Kalinowski had no success either, attacking him frontally, on the flanks, and rear, but were always repulsed. They attacked on 15 May 1651, near Zborov, and having attacked, among others, the Sobieski Regiment, they lost one of their colonels, Canowiecz, and a Tartar murza.

This general was finally constrained, because of bad passages and difficult roads, to abandon his wagons. To make up for this loss and to make his army seem larger than that of his enemies, he mounted his servants on the cart horses. Despite repeated attacks and difficulties while on his march, he ended it successfully by joining the Royal Army at the end of May.

The troops raised at the expense of the Republic and by the lords arrived from everywhere. Those raised by the latter came to 10,000 men and all joined to the nobility bringing the army's strength to at least 100,000 combatants, not including the servants, the number of which was very large. Most of the servants were armed and mounted. The number was so great that it would not long remain in one area before it stripped it of all resources and began to suffer from a lack of food and forage. As a result, the King, after issuing all the orders possible, so that nothing was lacking, resolved to immediately put it in movement. In the Great War Council, which was held, and which lasted a night, some of the nobles proposed dividing the army into two corps and sending one formed of the paid troops, against the enemy, while the King was to await the success of the war at Sokal, with the *arrière-ban*, as a reserve corps, to serve in the most pressing need. This advice was not to the King's taste, nor that of many of his officers, who noted that such a division would allow the detached corps to be enveloped and defeated by the Cossacks, while united it would not only be able to take the Cossacks on directly, but even to defeat them. It was concluded to march on the Cossacks by the shortest and easiest route, which was that to Beresteczko. The King took this route on 15 June with all the troops, after having detached various skirmishers to make contact with the Cossacks, and having recognized that the swamps that he would find while on his march and the innumerable quantity of wagons in his train, he divided his force into 10 brigades, each of 10,000 to 12,000 men.

The King took command of the first, which consisted of the professional troops. The second went to the Grand General (Grand Hetman) Potocki; the third to Général de Campagne (Field Hetman) Kalinowski, Palatine of Czernihovie; the fourth to Jan Simon Szcawinski, Palatine of Brescz; the fifth to the Duke of Wisnowiecz, Palatine of Russia; the sixth to Stanislaw Potocki, Palatine of Podolia; the seventh to Grand Marshal of the Kingdom Lubormirski; the eighth to Stanislaw Landskoronski, Palatine of Braclaw; the ninth to Vice-Chancellor of Lithuania Sapieha; and the tenth to Koniecpolski, Grand Ensign of the Crown. On the 16th, the Polish army moved to Wygnanka, an area with plentiful water and pastures. Here they learned the Cossack Army that Khmelnytsky had left his camp between Zbaras and Wiśniowiec and was moving on Cham from a soldier who had deserted. His army included a prodigious number of peasants that had joined his Cossacks, but so far he had only 6,000 Tartars.

The King arrived at Beresteczko, a city where the Count of Lesno, the Under Chamberlain of Brzesc was lord. He erected his camp near the city, along both sides of the Ster. He detached 3,000 horse, under Stemkowski and Czarnecki to gain firm information on the movement of the Cossacks. He learned from a few prisoners that the Tartar Cham had joined Khmelnytsky with a numerous army and that he had sent parties to learn of the location and state of the Polish army.

Upon learning of this the King held a council of war where it was decided to decamp the army, leave Beresteczko and move to Dubno, a city belonging to the Palatine of Cracow. The baggage had already begun to move and the army moved out resolved to engage the Cossacks wherever they found them, when the Prince of Wiśniowiec sent word to the King that Khmelnytsky and the Tartar Cham were marching directly against them. He was informed by the Grand General (Grand Hetman), who had learned of this from a peasant that the Cossacks promised victory if they engaged the Polish army on the road on which they were marching. He insisted in remaining at Beresteczko and called back the baggage, which had departed. They had barely re-entered the camp when the drummers on the towers announced that the Cossack and Tartar army was approaching from Pereatin, a village 500 paces from the city.

Immediately the King and the generals of the Polish army arranged their forces for battle, placing a flank on the

Styr River and filled all the copses nearby with platoons of infantry to prevent ambushes.

During the evening of 27 June, 10,000 Tartars detached from the main body approached the Polish army to execute a reconnaissance and determine if they wished to provoke a fight. The Grand Marshal and the Grand Ensign were unwilling to suffer their bravado and sortied, with the permission of the Grand General (Grand Hetman), with their regiments, supported by the Wiśniowiec Regiment. They fought with the Tartars for a long time and drove them back a half league. The 19th passed with an even harsher skirmish. The Tartar Khan had posted himself on a ridge with all his army, fortified by some chosen Cossack troops. The Polish army again went in battle formation, with the regiments of the Palatines of Brzesc and Pomerania, the Prince Bogusław Radziwiłł, and the Palatine of Vitebsk, and with the Premyśl and Volhynia Cavalry, advanced to charge the Tartars. The Tartars, seeing that this force was supported by few infantry, sought to take their revenge for the preceding day. They fell on the Poles with their heavy squadrons. Landskoronski stopped their first effort with heavy losses, including his brother. In the next attack the Poles were immediately enveloped by a large number of these infidels, so the main body found itself obliged to disengage from them and sent out the regiments of the Grand General (Grand Hetman), the General de Campagne (Field Hetman), the Palatine of Russia, the Grand Marshal, and Sapieha.

The battle renewed with the arrival of this reinforcement and many fell. The Tartars lost about 1,000 men and a few men of note were taken prisoner, including the Tartar Khan's secretary. However, the Poles lost 300 killed, including Casanowski, Castellan of Halicz; Ossoliński Starosta of Lublin, the nephew of the deceased Grand Chancellor; Standniski, Under Chamberlain of Sanoc; Ligeza, Sword Bearer Premyśl, Recziski, Knight Jourda, and several gentlemen from the Palatinate of Lenicice. Thus ended the day of 28 June. That evening, in a council of war, it was determined that the Cossacks wished to reduce the Poles to consuming their food and ruining them by holding them too far from a location from which they could draw sustenance. As a result, it was resolved to give battle the next day.

The King spent the best part of the night in his devotions and giving the necessary orders. When day broke, he arranged his army in battle, which the Cossacks could not observe, under the cover of a very thick fog, which lasted until 9:00 a.m. The right wing of the first line was commanded by Grand General Potocki, who had under him Landskoronski, Palatine of Braclaw; Opalinski, Palatine of Posnia; Lubomirski, Grand Marshal of the Kingdom; Sapieha, Vice Chancellor of Lithuania; Koniecpolski, Grand Hetman of the Crown; Count Władysław of Leszno, Under Chamberlain of Posnania; the two Sobieski sons of the deceased Castellan of Cracow and some other lords who had raised troops at their own expense.

The command of the left wing was given to General de Campagne (Field Hetman) Kalinowski, to the Dukes of Ostrog and Zaslaw, to the Palatine of Brzestye, the Prince of Wiśniowiec, Palatine of Russia; Stanislas Potocki, Palatine of Podolia; to Jan Zamoyski, and Colonel Jean d'Enhoff Lifflandois. Many of these men had joined troops raised in their lands to those of the Republic.

The King took command of the battle corps, containing all the German and Polish infantry, at the head of which was the artillery, under the command of Sigismund Priemski, who was [the artillery] General and who had long served as General Major in the Swedish army in Germany.

The second line, in the middle of which the King of Poland had placed his post, consisted solely of cavalry and was led by, among other officers, Tyskewitz, Grand Eschançon of Lithuania. The reserve corps was commanded by Colonel Meydel, Grand Huntsman, and Enhoff Starosta of Sokal. It consisted of their cavalry and that of Grudzinski and Rozaraevski, and the infantry of Prince Charles, brother of the King, of Koniecpolski, and the Frenchman, Colonel du Plessis. All the baggage was with the ammunition in the camp, which was covered by a trench on one side and covered on the other by the city and the river.

The King held back some troops in the camp as his guard. This force appeared more numerous than it really was because of the lances that the King had given to the hussars, which had a red battle pennant. They were arranged in battle formation and presented a wonderful picture.

The sun broke up the fog that had concealed the army. It was as if a curtain had been raised in a theater, exposing the Polish army to their enemies, who were surprised to see such a large force.

The Cossack and Tartar army totaled more than 300,000 combatants which covered more ground than could be seen. The Tartars, who had seized some neighboring heights with a very gentle slope, were formed in a crescent. They had the Cossacks on their right, who were opposite the left wing of the Polish army, in which were intermixed with squadrons of Tartars. Nearby there was the Cossack *tabor [wagen laager]* which was formed of several ranks of wagons, in the middle of which was part of their forces. In this position, they were capable of withstanding all sorts of attacks.

The two armies were thus arranged, while all the morning was spent in little skirmishes. The King believed it was the Cossacks' intentions to amuse him with little skirmishes during the day and then attack him during the night figuring that they could better surprise him under the cover of darkness. He prohibited his soldiers, on pain of death, from leaving their posts without orders and broke all the bridges over the Ster River in order that he could not be attacked from the rear. This was also so that his army would have to fight or die. So as to usefully employ the rest of the day, of which not enough remained to handle a general battle between the two armies totaling over 400,000, he began firing salvos of his cannon over the heads of his men against the enemy to the measure that his troops approached the heights occupied by the Tartars. Many seeing that the day was so advanced wished that the battle would be resumed the next day. Others insisted, to the contrary, fearing that the Cossacks would fall on the Polish army with their *tabor*, which they had extraordinarily reinforced, did not wish to abandon the battlefield to them.

At this point the King issued the order for the Prince of Wiśniowiec to begin the battle. He had 12 companies of veteran troops and was supported by the Palatine of Podolia, with the *arrière-ban* of the Palatinates of Cracow, Sandomierz, Legnica, and Przemysl. The Cossacks received them with a very sharp countercharge and the melee lasted for nearly an hour. During this engagement the smoke and dust concealed from sight the various troops. As one Polish troop began to fold it was supported by fresh troops that the King sent forward. The Cossacks were pushed into their tabor [wagen laager] and the Tartars were pushed back to the heights. The King then marched with his battle against the main body of the Tartars, the right wing being stopped near a wood to block the design of many of the enemy that were concealed there in ambush, with the intention of enveloping the Polish army when it was tied down in a melee.

The King, who pushed his artillery before him and General Priemski fired constantly and with much success. Together they drove the Tartars away from the base of the mountain and, by degrees seized the summit, after having suffered the fire of the muskets of the Janissaries, who accompanied them.

The King, who was present at this part of the battlefield, was in great personal danger. Four balls from the cannon that the Tartars had in the edge of the wood passed near them and one fell at his feet. The Polish immediately responded as Otuinovski, the King's interpreter of the Turkish and Tartar languages, had assured him that the Tartar Khan was there in person, at the point where they saw a great white standard. The King had a cannon fired in that direction and the first shot cut down one of the principal Tartar officers, who was near the Khan. The Khan was forced to retire. The Tartar army, which had been pushed off the mountain, left a few squadrons behind to cover its retreat and to amuse the Poles for some time. This rearguard soon withdrew and was pursued for a league and a half until the night and the speed of their *bacmates*[3] put them in safety. In their retreat, however, they abandoned many of their dead and wounded, which they normally carried away and burned during their march, when they had the leisure to do so, which was considered an abomination. They also abandoned much of their equipment, such as jackets, saddles, sabers, wagons, tents, as well as the Khan's standard and his silver drum. Several Poles, who were slaves of the infidels, recovered their liberty, but

---

[3]Bacmates – Tartar name for their horses.

many were massacred when it became apparent that they could not be carried away during their retreat. By the arrival of the morning they had moved 10 French leagues from the battlefield.

After having detached various bodies of cavalry to pursue the Tartars, the King ordered the rest of his forces to surround the Cossack *tabor*. There were still 200,000 Cossacks, with 40 cannon, which executed a continual fire.

Khmelnytsky had retired with the Tartars with the intention of re-engaging them in the battle, but he could not persuade them. To the contrary, he was abused by the words of the Khan, who reproached him for having concealed the state of the Polish army from him, telling him that it contained only 20,000 men. The Khan threatened to send him to the King of Poland in exchange for the *murzas* that he held prisoner.

The Khan did not wish to let Khmelnytsky go and so Khmelnytsky sent orders to Czeherin to send him a large sum of money as well as part of the booty that had been taken in Poland.

The King of Poland, by the grace of God, held the battlefield and won the victory. It had cost him 1,200 men and the Cossacks and Tartars were believed to have lost six times more than that. He spent the night in his tent, during which it rained so heavily that he could not move his cannon up the mountain abandoned by the Tartars so he could fire on the Cossack *tabor*.

The Cossacks had surrounded their *tabor* with a wide and deep ditch and put musketeers at the weakest and most open points. They had a great swamp to their rear which assured them entirely. In the absence of Khmelnytsky, command of their army fell to one of their officers named Dzhalalii, who was well-known for his cruelty.

Having taken all steps possible to procure their safety, they called on the King for his clemency and expressed their extreme desire for peace. However, as they had taken up arms, at the same time as they had taken up the pen, their letters were rejected and the King thought only of reducing them by force and even more so as he learned they were beginning to fracture.

Some officers were of the opinion that they should flood the Cossack camp by damming up a nearby stream, but it was decided to pound them to ruin with the Polish cannon and to that end the heavy cannon from the Brody fortress were brought up. The Poles also prepared posts above and below their camp for communication of within their lines; constructing many forts and redoubts on the high points to receive these cannon.

On 4 July, the Cossacks surprised one of these forts where there were two cannon and 80 Poles on guard. They cut down the survivors with their scythes, a weapon that their soldiers normally carried in lieu of pikes. General Hubald rushed up and chased them away, but they still succeeded in dragging the Polish cannon back to their *tabor*. That same day they captured a hill in order to make foraging easier. The Poles drove them back and captured 500 of their horses. On the 5th, they came out of their camp in great numbers and caused the Poles to believe that they were about to renew the battle, but the Cossacks were driven back into their trenches after a rough battle, in which they lost 400 men. Sokol and Piasoczin were wounded on the Polish side, in this melee. After the fight both sides settled down into an artillery duel.

The Cossacks, seeing themselves in a bad position, now sought to employ a ruse by attacking, the Polish army with all their forces the next night in the hopes of destroying them. However, their plan was betrayed by the rain and then by the vigilance of the King and his generals, who had doubled their guards. However, Mehmet Czelebey, a Polish Tartar, who for a long time had been in the service of the Grand Hetman, who had made him a captain, and had been sent out with a party to pursue the Tartars, now returned to the camp, bringing a Tartar prisoner named Murtasa Aga, a relative of Cha. He had been wounded in the battle of Beresteczko and was unable to follow his men. He offered Czelebey a ransom of 15,000 Reichsthalers. Czelebey, however, offered his fealty to the Grand Hetman - his master over the money and the other advantages that the Tartar lord had promised him, if he returned him to his land. He reported that he had found more than 1,000 dead or mortally wounded Tartars along the road, who had been abandoned by their fellow Tartars. This was an extraordinary situation, as it was their custom to burn them instead of abandoning their dead to their enemies.

The Cossacks, whose last plan had failed, now found themselves more tightly pressed and at a serious disadvantage. The only recourse that remained to them was to escape through the swamp. However, Colonel Balban, who was posted with 1,000 men on the other side of the water, had begun to block this route. It was then decided to send a large number of Polish troops to that side of the swamp so as to entirely seal off this passage.

Finally, the Polish artillery began pounding the enemy *tabor* with a grand bombardment. The Cossacks responded by sending out three of their deputies: Kresa (colonel of the Czeherin Regiment), Hladki, and Pereaslavski, to ask for peace. Initially they spoke to the Grand General (Grand Hetmans), who reproached them for their cruelty and perfidy. He told that they were unworthy of the grace of His Polish Majesty and that they did not merit being treated as Christians, after their infamous alliance with the

Turks and the Tartars.

Nonetheless the King, upon the advice of some senators, admitted them to an audience, under a tent erected on the mountain, from which the Tartars had been driven. They prostrated themselves before the King, presenting to him a letter in the name of all the Cossacks, asking him repeatedly for forgiveness, repeating these words to all the demands made to them, kissing the hands and robes of the senators who were present. His Polish Majesty held a conference with his inner circle and responded to them by the Bishop of Kulm, his Grand Chancellor, that as terrible as their crimes had been, which should have stripped them of any hope of pardon, His Majesty desired to conform to divine goodness and mercy, and would forgive them providing that they would give sufficient proofs of a true repentance and a perfect submission. They were to give this to him in writing the next day at 11 o'clock. Until that time there was to be a suspension of arms and Cresa, their principal deputy would remain as a hostage. The other deputies returned on the 7th, at the indicated hour, to receive the articles by which His Polish Majesty granted them what they had requested.

This document said in the following articles:

1. That they would give 12 of their principal officers as hostages, including General Khmelnytsky and Wikowski, his secretary;
2. That they return the artillery and flags that they had captured during this war;
3. That they would hand over the standard of the general of their militia (Cossack Hetman); which would then be given to whomever the King might choose;
4. That they would be reduced to 12,000 registered Cossacks, who would serve to guard the frontier and

that this article would be submitted to the next Diet;
5.) That with regard to the privileges that they might claim, they would have only those granted to them in 1648 by the deceased General Koniecpolski.

The Cossack deputies returned to their camp and read out the conditions. The next day they gave their response. With regards to the first article, they promised to do everything they could to place Khmelnytsky and his secretary in the King's hands, but they would not give any hostages for this purpose; that they would accept the second and third points, and that for the rest, that they would only accept the conditions established by the Treaty of Zboriv.

The King was offended by this response and redoubled his batteries, resolving to exterminate the Cossacks. The Cossacks, preferring death to abandoning their rights under the Treaty of Zboriv, returned fire with their cannon to the Polish cannon, but they soon began to run out of gunpowder. Some Cossacks were so bold that they moved close to the Polish camp, where they heard the order being given to the soldiers, by the trumpets. Realizing their plan was betrayed, the Poles abandoned their plan for an immediate assault on the Cossack *tabor*. The Cossacks resisted all efforts made by the Poles against them and their valor would have earned them great praise if it had not been accompanied by many detestable cruelties that they inflicted on the Poles that fell into their hands and were tortured. The conditions being imposed on them for peace had inspired them to a fury and their *Poppes* [priests] promised them the prompt return of their general and the Tartars. However, their suffering and the long absence of their general stripped them of any hope of any prompt relief. The Cossack multitude now began to ask that the peace offer be accepted. Their leaders resisted this with all their power, and upon seeing that Dzhalalii, who had replaced Khmelnytsky, was looking favorably on accepting these conditions, removed him and put Bohun in his place.

Bohun, to demonstrate his command and knowing that the Palatine of Braclaw had crossed some troops over the river to close the passages over which the Cossacks were accustomed to forage and by which he would have to retire, he sent a large number of the old Cossack Militia and two cannon to drive them away and to reinforce the guards of the forts that they had constructed to defend this passage. However, these men had barely left the camp than the rumor spread that they and their leaders were retiring and planned on abandoning the others. Chaos erupted and everyone began to flee.

The paths that they had constructed through the swamps near their camp were too narrow and many tumbled into the swamp, being unable to extract themselves. The Cossacks threw away their weapons and equipment. Bohun saw this confusion and ran to his veteran soldiers to remedy the problem, but the torrent of fleeing soldiers swept them away as well.

The Palatine of Braclaw, who had a view of the Cossack Army, could not imagine what was happening. He believed that they were moving to fall on him, so he posted himself with the 2,000 men he had with him, in a position where they could not be enveloped. However, as he got a better view and understanding of the Cossack activities, he changed his mind and moved to follow them. He was, however, stopped by a defile, through which they Cossacks were fleeing. He attacked the Cossacks, supported by the *arrière-ban* of the Palatinate of Polsko, which was nearby. The rest of the Polish army, which had not expected such a sudden rout of the Cossacks were not mounted and only the camp reserve was ready to move. The reserve moved to the right of the camp where it encountered a mass of booty. Instead of pushing into the tabor and attacking, they turned to looting.

Many Cossacks escaped, but not without leaving 20,000 dead, either killed by the Poles or dying in the brush and swamp. Two thousand of them withdrew to a small hill inside the *tabor* resolved to defend themselves and sell their lives as dearly as possible. Seeing that they would be overwhelmed many jumped into the river while others ran into the swamp.

Another group of 300 Cossacks defended themselves valiantly against a great number of attackers, who pressed them on all sides. The Poles promised to spare them, but they refused. The Cossacks then emptied their pockets and belts of all their money and threw them into the river. Eventually, however, they were all killed in single combat in a fight that lasted for three hours.

One Cossack found a small boat by a lake in the swamp and defended himself there until he ran out of powder. He then used his scythe driving back all who attempted to attack him. A Muscovite attacked him with the same weapon and held him at bay. Meanwhile a gentleman from Czechanov and a German infantryman, not judging that the Muscovite would prevail, moved into the water up to the neck and having resumed the battle, the Cossack was shot by fourteen musket shots, which the Cossack shrugged off, to the great astonishment of the army and the Polish King, who was watching the fight. The King, admiring the Cossack's valor, cried out to him, offering him his life if he would surrender. The Cossack responded that he did not care to live but would prefer to die as a true soldier. At that point he was struck by a pike blow by another German soldier who had come up to join the battle.

In the Cossack camp, the Poles found, in addition to a large number of women and children, a considerable booty. This included 40 cannon, among which were 18 battery guns, much powder, and many flags, including the standard that the King had sent to General Khmelnytsky upon his election to mark his confirmation in the Hetmanate. They found another that the deceased King Władysław had sent to the Cossacks, when he was meditating a war against the Muscovites and another that the Cossacks had taken from the Poles on 25 June, the sword that the Greek Patriarch had given to Khmelnytsky in recognition of his acceptance of the Orthodox Religion, chapel ornaments and other precious furniture that a Greek Prelate called the Archbishop of Corinth, and who had remained with Khmelnytsky on the behest of the Patriarch. He was one of the men who had most inspired the revolt among the Cossacks and Russians, and who was most opposed to accepting the terms proposed by the King of Poland. He had been killed by an arrow fired by the Poles during the rout. They also found Khmelnytsky's chest, which contained the seal of the Zaporozhian Army, various letters from the Great Lord [Sultan], the Grand Duke of Moscow, and the Prince of Transylvania. They also found about 30,000 Reichsthalers, which were intended for the Tartars, vests lined with valuable furs, a large number of weapons, and an abundance of food. They also found pots and spits on the fires, which were certain proof that the flight had not been premeditated, but that it was an act of God.

In this battle the Poles lost only a few men and a captain of the Radziwill Infantry Regiment, who was killed in the attack of the 300 Cossacks retiring through the swamp. In addition to those who had been sent in pursuit of the Cossacks, Général de Campagne (Field Hetman) and the

Prince of Wiśniowiec were detached with seven regiments to prevent the Cossacks from rallying. They cut down all that they encountered on the roads. A large part of Cossacks retired thru Dubno, 3,000 were torn to pieces by the garrison of that city and some troops sent in that direction, as they moved along the levy. Almost all the arrière-ban that the King had left at Beresteczko, marched towards Krzemieniecz at the same time. Along this route he found many horrible sights, the roads being covered with dead bodies and the woods filled with miserable men, who after their rout had fled into the deep forests and had nothing to eat after a few days except tree bark. They were so weak they were no longer able to flee. The indignation of the Poles changed to pity, at the sight of these skeletons and, instead of killing them, they only acted to rescue them. The King also had the grace, that upon seeing them in this state, to have food distributed to them and assuring them of a royal pardon if they left the rebels and returned to their homes.

In his clemency, the King also realized that the rebellious population had desolated one of the principal provinces of his kingdom, which served as a rampart to others and had ruined the lands of many of the great lords, who could not draw any revenues from depopulated lands. The serfs were part of the inheritances and if the land was stripped of them, they could only be replaced with the greatest difficulty. This was the true reason for this policy and many other actions that prevented the complete destruction of the Cossacks.

The King judged his presence necessary for the termination of this war and to achieve the reduction of the Cossacks, looking to move with his army to Kiev, from where he sent the troops and orders necessary to execute this plan. However, the nobility resisted, alleging that they had to return to their homes to attend to business. They claimed that the *arrière-ban* would be sufficient as the Cossacks were dispersed and in no condition to recover from their retreat. If some of them were inclined to take up arms, the mercenary troops would be sufficient to prevent this and make all their efforts useless. In a word, there was no reason to take the nobility into a land that was abandoned and desolated by the Cossacks and Tartars where they might die of hunger.

A council of war was held at Orla that was attended by all the leaders and officers of the army. It was necessary to surrender to their opinion and to allow those who wished to leave, and it was a very large number of them, to go.

The King, after having given his orders to Grand General Potocki, continue in the path outlined, took the road to Warsaw, having obtained before his departure, the word of the nobility that they would provide a new force of men and money.

Before leaving the army the King received word that the Tartar Khan, learning of the rout of the Cossacks, had halted his retreat towards the Crimea and that he had been reinforced by 4,000 Turks. The Khan then re-crossed the Dnieper. This news was accompanied by news of the defeat of the Cossacks in Lithuania by Prince Radziwiłł.

Twelve thousand Cossacks, commanded by their general named Niababy, were posted near Loiovogrod, at the confluence of the Sož River and the Dnieper. After constructing some works to assure the passage of these rivers, the general left there troops to garrison them. Prince Radziwiłł, General of Lithuania (Grand Hetman of Lithuania), resolved to force them, after having sent, to this end, before them, General Major Mirski with 3,000 chosen men, to whom he had given orders to cross to the far bank of the

Dnieper. He then moved with the rest of his men and his artillery down the river, while his cavalry moved alongside it. After his arrival he attacked the entrenchments on one side while Mirski, to whom he had given the signal by some cannon volleys, attacked the other.

The Cossacks defended themselves bravely for an hour and a half, after which they were broken and scattered. Niababy hurried to the relief of his men with his army. Although Mirski hadn't arrived yet from across, Prince Radziwiłł engaged the enemy. After a tremendous charge, in which three of the principal Cossack colonels (polkovnyks) and General Niababy, were killed, this army was defeated. Three thousand Cossacks were killed and many were taken prisoners, including Niababy's nephew. The rest saved themselves by fleeing to their camp, which was not far and was subsequently abandoned. Christophle Potocki, Assistant Steward of Lithuania, sent a detachment to reconnoiter it.

The Cossacks had also abandoned the cities of Lubiecz and Chornobyl upon the approach of Gosiewski, General of the Lithuanian Artillery, without much resistance. After this Prince Radziwiłł took the road to Kiev to complete the ruin of the remains of the revolt in that region.

General Potocki occupied himself with doing the same in Volhynia, where the difficulty of obtaining food and forage had obliged him to separate his army into several corps. He gave them as a rendezvous the city of Lubartów, a city which by its situation and the number of its inhabitants had survived unscathed during this war. Potocki sought to move, from there, and strike Pawolocz and Bialacierkiev. He recommended to all his officers to feed their soldiers in such a manner that the peasants were not obliged, by their bad treatment, to abandon their homes and to not spoil what remained of their food and forage. Their lords also took care to return them to their duty, promising them by letters and express messages, a favorable treatment, provided they saw the error of their ways.

Meanwhile, Khmelnytsky, by means of a sum of money with which he had appeased the Tartar Khan, had escaped his hands and returned to the Ukraine to bolster the morale of the people which was greatly shaken by his set-backs and absence. He made rousing speeches and employed, in places where he could not go, his pen and emissaries to fire up their courage and to exhort them to support the common cause. He continued to remind them that Fortune was fickle and there would be setbacks, which if they had recently declared in favor of the Poles, the Cossacks still contained enough vigor and sufficient forces to renew the war and to replace their losses. News came that a certain Rákóczi, had moved on Poland and that this had obliged the King to send the large part of his army to stop his progress. He stated that the flower of the old Cossack Militia was assembling and that in a few days the Tartars would rejoin them in order to gain the revenge for their recent defeat. In addition, to maintain the hopes of the people who served him, he dispatched ambassadors to the Khan from time to time, who sent back magnificent promises to send him new relief. Khmelnytsky reminded the Khan that his security depended on his fortune and that the destruction of the Cossacks would only lead to the Tartar's destruction by the Poles. He also sent three deputies to the Porte to ask for help and to represent that if the Cossacks were assisted by the Great Lord, they would be in a state to face all the forces of Poland. On the other hand, they said to the Great Lord [Sultan] that if he abandoned him, they would be obliged to come to an accommodation with the Poles and that eventually there would be a war.

Meanwhile, the Palatine of Smolensk, Helbowitz, had joined Prince Janusz Radziwiłł, but left a lieutenant colonel of a hussar unit named Fronckewitz, , with some troops around Czernichów to contain raids of the city's garrison. He then moved towards Kiev after having driven away Cossack Colonels Antoine and Orkussa, and put their troops in such disorder that after burning their *tabor* and their bridge, they were obliged to retire. However, they did not stay away long although the fear of the approaching Lithuanian army spread throughout the other Cossack troops, who thought themselves in safety. They abandoned the city, which was one of their principal retreats. The inhabitants of the city, finding themselves stripped of their garrisons and any other source of defense, took recourse to making overtures to the Polish generals by means of their archbishop and the Archimandrite[4], to spare their city, which the King had always had the goodness to adhere to, as he had, during the Azyle's wars against the Polish nobility. Their prayers were heard and Prince Radziwiłł contented himself with disarming the people so as to deny them the means of doing any ill in the future.

Khmelnytsky, having learned of the loss of Kiev, redoubled his efforts and employed every means possible to reconstitute a new army corps capable of stopping the progress of his enemies. The bad state of his affairs suggested to him the full councils of fury and disappointment. He found not only his Cossacks, but part of the peasants were disposed to again tempt the fate on the battlefield and he encountered among the latter those that exclaimed loudly that it was an infamous loss of courage that caused them to lose the battle when some troops fled. There were others that said a similar disgrace could strike them. These

---

[4]A senior abbot who assists the bishop.

said that if fortune persisted in holding with the Poles, they would have to retreat into the lands of the Turks, where they could live with more freedom and sweetness than in Russia, and that they had already written to the Bassa of Silistria to that end.

More and more peasants joined Khmelnytsky daily however, so the Cossacks resumed their raids and ravages in various places, particularly those that were bordering the Niestra and the Wallachian's, who were more accustomed to brigandage than the others. General Potocki had detached 2,000 men, under the command of the Starosta of Kamianets, who was his son, to disperse the raiders. However, he soon recalled his son. Instead of sending him the support he had requested, judging it more appropriate to reassemble all his troops into a single corps. He did, however, send seven squadrons towards Bila Tserkvo to make contact with the Cossacks. Instead of executing the orders they had been given, they amused themselves with pillaging Pawołocz. They were caught near there by 2,000 Cossacks and 500 Tartars, who charging, defeated them, and pursued them to the gates of Pawołocz after they were forced to abandon their booty. Their defeat would have been inevitable had not the Prince of Wiśniowiec arrived. The pursued became the pursuers and pushed part of the Cossack-Tartar force into their *tabor* and the others to Bila Tserkvo. They learned from some Tartar prisoners that were taken on this occasion, that there were only 2,000 Tartars with Khmelnytsky, but that he would be joined, in a few days, by 4,000 more. As for the rest of the Tartars, they had gone to pasture their horses in the deserted plains and had received orders to hold themselves ready to return to Poland. This news obliged General Potocki to stop his march until his baggage and infantry had arrived. After this he deliberated with his officers what to do. It was resolved to seize Chwastowa, a city on the road to Kiev, both to facilitate his communication and his junction with Prince Radziwiłł.

While Potocki was encamped at Pawołocz, waiting for his infantry, which was marching very slowly, a contagious disease took Jeremi Wiśniowieki, Prince of Wiśniowiec, who had given repeated proofs of his valor and a singular conduct during all of this war, which had taken from him all his properties located in the Ukraine.[5]

After the army gave him their last salute, on 25 August, they marched the next day towards the well-fortified city of Trylisicz. The garrison responded with a proud "no," when the general called on them to surrender. As a result Radziwiłł ordered Priemski, the General of Artillery, the Commissioner of the Army, and Berg, lieutenant colonel of the Prince Bogusław Radziwiłł Regiment, with 700 German infantry, to attack the city. They lost 60-80 men in the approaches, including Captains Strausse and Wahl, but being reinforced by some Polish Infantry, they took the city and its castle in less than two hours, notwithstanding a most stubborn resistance by the besieged. Even the women of the city fought with scythes. Everyone was put to the sword without distinction of age or sex. The Cossack governor was hung and after that the city was put to pillage, then burned.

This harsh treatment had an immediate effect, because the fire having been seen by those at Chwstowa, the 300 Cossacks that guarded that city abandoned it and the inhabitants followed their example, even though they might have fought the Poles and inflicted a good number of casualties on them.

Prince Janusz Radziwiłł waited for orders from the King and the approach of the Polish army while he main-

---

[5]Probably cholera

tained himself near Kiev even though he was in some danger. The Cossacks sought every means possible to surprise him or at least to prevent his junction with General Potocki.

On 16 August, Colonel Nold was sent by this prince who found near a mill that was very close to the Golden Gate of Kiev a mixed body of Cossacks and Tartars. The alarm was given in the camp and a body of light cavalry pushed them so hard that more than 1,000 were left on the field. It was learned from some prisoners that the main body, of 3,000 men, was to be supported by 1,000 others, with the idea of forcing the Lithuanian army into its entrenchments.

With this victory in hand, Prince Radziwill raised his pikes and marched to join the Polish army after leaving a sufficient garrison in Kiev and having taken the steps necessary to assure its protection. General Potocki, sent an advanced force of 1,500 men before marching to Vasilikow with the rest of the army to facilitate this junction. Khmelnytsky was powerless to prevent this and realizing the severity of his situation sent deputies to the Polish general to speak with him of a truce and to use his influence in the Senate and within the armies of the Republic in order to prevent an effusion of blood that was coming as well as to put him and his Cossacks back into the good graces of the King of Poland, assuring that they remained faithful to his service and religiously executed the Treaty of Zboriv. This peace proposal put forward by Khmelnytsky did not make a great impression on the spirit of the Polish general, who was well-informed of the continual contact between Khmelnytsky with the Porte as well as the Tartar Khan to support him. As a result of that, Potocki realized that these peace feelers were only an effort to gain time and allow Khmelnytsky to re-establish his affairs. He determined not to stop, but to end this war by force. The Polish army was now notably reinforced by the junction of a Lithuanian army of 9,000 men. However, Khmelnytsky was not discouraged, receiving a reinforcement of 6,000 Tartars and made a new attempt to obtain a truce. The Palatine of Kiev also attempted to persuade these generals to accept the Cossack proposal and bring an end to the war - be it by a pardon or by a continuation or by the death of the soldiers. He argued that each day they continued the campaign they lost soldiers to fatigue and sickness. These arguments convinced Generals Potocki and Radziwiłł to receive the Cossack deputies who came to request a peace. Khmelnytsky requested that someone be sent to him to discuss the conditions of peace with his subordinate and principal confident, Vyhovsky. To this end, Makowski, captain of cavalry, was given a letter from General Potocki for him. However, as he did not give him the respect due a General of the Zaporozhian Army, this omission was taken as a great insult and initially created a great deal of unrest among the Cossacks. Makowski then apologized and appeased them. At the opening of negotiations the Polish deputy proposed that Khmelnytsky dismiss the Tartars and return to his allegiance to Poland as one of their generals. Khmelnytsky long resisted the first of these propositions, something which his commander knew he would not accept. In the end nothing was resolved. The officers and Russian peasants were very upset at the latter. Not finding it appropriate to continue negotiations in the camp and fearing that the Tartars had doubts about what was being negotiated, Vyhovsky suggested that they move the conference to the city of Bila Tserkvo.

Makowski, reported about his negotiations with the Cossacks to the generals of the Polish army and it was decide to send some commissioners to Bila Tserkvo, as had been requested. For this purpose, they deputized the Palatines of Kiev and Smolensk, Gosiewski Grand Steward of Lithuania, and Kossakowski Voivode of Bracław, to whom they gave a strong escort, of which only 500 were allowed to enter the city. The commissioners joined Khmelnytsky's commissioners, continuing to work on all the conditions of the peace, reserving some that would be voted on later in the camps. The Polish deputies, however, were in danger for their lives, primarily from the Cossack Army where Khmelnytsky and his colonels could barely control the Tartars and the peasants, who hated the thought of any peace proposition. They feared that any treaty would once again reduce them to servitude. The Tartars proved to be beyond control and pillaged part of their baggage.

Meanwhile, General Potoski and Prince Janusz Radziwiłł, seeing that these negotiations were nearly completed, advanced from Hermanowka where they were posted, towards Bila Tserkvo, which was the location where Khmelnytsky and the principal Cossack leaders were to renew their oath to the King and the Republic.

The Cossacks were disturbed by the approach of the Polish army, but it had been represented to them that this movement had no other intent than to oppose new raids by the Tartars. New commissioners were sent back and forth to resolve points that were still unresolved in the Bila Tserkvo conference.

The Cossacks, instead, made totally new propositions as if they had lost the memory of what had been already agreed upon, asking for the execution of the Treaty of Zboriv; the withdrawal of the Republic's army to the frontier, the liberty to maintain their alliance with the Tartars, which they saw as the true defenders of their liberty. After being reproached for this behavior and their lack of faith, which was apparently provoked by the Tartars, or a false rumor of troops coming from Turkey, the Polish generals arranged their armies for battle, the right wing being under Prince Radziwiłł with the Lithuanian troops, the left under the Field Hetman Kalinowski, and General Potocki commanded the battle. The Cossacks and Tartars came out of their camp, appearing to have no other plan than to observe the disposition of the Poles. Several skirmishes occurred over the next three days and many Cossacks and Tartars concealed themselves in the brush and covered places, making frequent attacks on the Polish army, harassing its flanks and rear. It was thought that they were doing this to encourage the Polish generals to be more generous in their negotiations and to obtain more advantageous conditions. On 26 September Khmelnytsky sent three deputies to them to work seriously on the conclusion of the treaty. Many of their conditions were accepted, but they were different from those that had been determined at Bila Tserkvo. After agreeing that there would be 20,000 enrolled Cossacks they requested that their quarters be in the Palatinates of Bracłav and Chernihiv. At first this was refused, so the Cossacks insisted that at least the Polish troops not be lodged there while Khmelnytsky was occupied in enrolling the registered Cossacks and that he be given, for his maintenance, the territories of Czyrcassy and Borowica. Potocki informed them that he could not grant them this request, without express orders from the King and the Republic.

Potocki later admitted to Khmelnytsky that he had been ordered to go there to contain the rebelling peasants; that he would not anger them as long as they were assembled and in large numbers. He believed that things were now resolved between them and it only remained for Khmelnytsky and his colonels to submit to the generals of the Republic's armies. Khmelnytsky agreed on the condition that sufficient hostages be provided to assure his safety. Some of his officers initially refused to accept these terms, but this was resolved and Khmelnytsky came to the Polish camp with his principal officers on 28 September. Once there these men humbly asked for grace from Grand Hetman Potocki, with tears in their eyes, and then saluted, with respect Prince Radziwiłł and the other lords. In his presence the terms of the treaty were read out. It was signed by both parties and confirmed with an oath. The signing ended with an ample banquet.

The articles of the treaty were:

First, in consideration of the submission made by the Zaporozhian army and the officers that commanded it, it will perpetually be attached to the service of the King and the Republic. That this army should be composed of, in the future, 20,000 men, who shall be chosen and enlisted by its general and his officers. That it shall have its quarters in the domains belonging to His Majesty, in the Palatines of Kiev, Braclaw, and Czernihow, and that those lands belonging to the nobility shall be restored.

2.) That if some subjects of this nobility were enrolled in the Zaporozhian Army, they shall be obliged to transfer their homes to the lands of the King in the Palatinate of Kiev and they shall be free to sell their goods, movable and unmovable, as they may, without being prevented in doing so by their lords, Starostas, or Assistant-Starostas.

3.) That one would begin making a roll of the 24,000 Cossacks retained on the 15th, to count from the signing of the present treaty, and that this roll or register, which shall contain the name, surname, and residence of each Cossack, and shall be signed by the General of the Cossacks, then shall be sent to the King and that it will remain in the Kiev Archives. That those who shall be incorporated shall enjoy the ancient rights and privileges of the Cossacks and shall pay the rents that they were earlier obliged to pay to the King.

4.) That the Polish armies cannot have their quarters in the Palatinate of Kiev or the locations designated for those of the Cossacks, and that they shall not take theirs in the Palatinates of Braclaw and Czernihow, after the festivals of Christmas, at which time the registration shall stop.

5.) That the gentlemen of said Palatinates of Kiev, Braclaw, and Czernihow shall be able to freely retake possession of their goods or Starostas and to draw the revenues as before, but they may not demand any fees or payments from their subjects, until after the formation of the register; the result of which it will be known who may truly enjoy the privileges of the Cossacks or to be excluded from them.

6.) That the General (Hetman) of Cossacks would have the city of Czerin for his maintenance and that Bogdan Khmelnytsky's successors will enjoy the prerogatives assigned to, shall confer the duties of other officers of this army and shall remain under the protection of the generalissimos of the Crown, to whom he is obliged by oath to maintain an inviable fidelity.

7.) That the Greek Orthodox Religion that the Zaporozhian Army professes shall be maintained in its ancient liberties, with all the dependent bishoprics, monasteries, and churches and that the ecclesiastic goods, which may have been usurped during course of this war shall be restored.

8.) That the Catholic or Greek nobility which has followed the Cossack party, as well as the inhabitants of Kiev shall enjoy amnesty and shall, in consequence, be re-established in all their goods, rights, honors, and liberties, and the condemnations, which may have been laid against them, on the occasion of this war, shall become null.

9.) That the Jews shall be maintained in the right of bourgeoisie, in the domains of the King and the lands of the gentlemen, and shall be assured of their goods and rights, as earlier.

10.) That the Tartars who are in the Kingdom, shall leave at the earliest moment without doing any damage and shall not have any quarter there, in any location whatever. That the General (Hetman) of the Cossacks shall do all he can in order to engage them to remain in the service of the Republic, but that it cannot come to an end until the next Diet when he and his Cossacks shall renounce their love of and their making of war, as enemies of the King and the Republic, that in addition they shall form no league, nor maintain any correspondence with any neighboring prince, but shall remain in a perpetual and constant fidelity and obedience towards His Majesty and the Republic; that they and their successors shall give marks on all occasions where they are commanded for his service.

11.) That as there have never been Cossacks enrolled for the guard of the Lithuanian frontier, and there shall never be, but they shall live as it was said in the limits of the Palatinate of Kiev.

12.) As said city of Kiev was a metropolitan and had a Justice Tribunal it shall enroll few Cossacks.

13.) As for the great security of this treaty, be it the Polish commissioners or the General of the Zaporozhian Army and its other leaders, they shall be obliged by an oath to its observation, after which the Polish army shall retire to its quarters there to await until after the soldiers that shall form the Zaporozhian Army have been selected and registered, and the Tartars have returned to their homes and the Cossacks equally to their homes.

14.) That Khmelnytsky and the Zaporozhian Army shall send deputies to the next Diet to thank most humbly the King and the Republic for the grace that has been given to them.

Shortly after this peace, Grand Hetman Potocki died of apoplexy in the city of Chmielnik, broken by age, but still more by the fatigues of war, which he had learned under the famous General (Hetman) Zolkiewitz. He had been in poor health since his imprisonment by the Tartars, but his great courage caused him to decline the remedies necessary for the re-establishment of his health, and sought, as he avowed confidentially to his friends, to die in war and doing his duty; in order that his wishes should be accomplished and in addition the satisfaction of ending his life so gloriously, as he had had done before his death, brought to an end by his valor in a war that was so cruel and ruinous to his homeland.

THE END

Bohdan Khmelnytsky (Bohdan Khmelnytsky or Khmelnitsky) (1595-1657)
Military and Political Leader of the Ukrainian Cossacks

Pierre Chevalier

Biography of Bohdan Khmelnytsky

Bohdan Khmelnytsky (or in Ukrainian Bohdan Zinovly Mykhaylovych Khmelnytsky), born 1595 in Chigirin, Ukraine, died 16 August 1657), organized a rebellion against Polish rule in the Ukraine that ultimately led to the transfer of the Ukrainian lands east of the Dnieper River from Polish to Russian rule.

Khmelnytsky was educated in Poland and served in the Polish army in its wars against the Turks. He became chief of the Cossacks at Czyhryn. As a result of a quarrel with the Polish governor of that region he was forced to flee, in December 1647, to the fortress of the Zaporozhian Cossacks, a semi-military community that had formed from runaway serfs, bandits, and traders who had settled on the Dnieper River.

Khmelnytsky subsequently organized the rebellion discussed in this work with the Zaporozhian Cossacks and marched against the Poles in April 1648. His initial victories won him support among dissatisfied peasants, townspeople, and the clergy of Ukraine. This led to an invasion of Poland proper and the capture of Lowo in October 1648. After a number of victories, in 1649 he signed a peace with the new Polish king John Casimir, where the Compact of Zboriv (18 August 1648) was signed. This compact allowed him to establish an almost totally independent Cossack principality in the Ukraine. Unfortunately, this treaty did not satisfy either the Polish gentry or Khmelnytsky's followers, as many of the latter remained under the control of Polish landlords.

The war erupted anew in 1651 and was defeated in the battle of Beresteczko in June. The subsequent treaty was far less advantageous to the Cossacks, so Khmelnytsky sought support from Moscow. In 1654, three years after the end of the events described in this book, he directed his Cossacks to take an oath of allegiance to Alexis, Tsar of Russia, in the Pereyaslav Agreement.

Even though the Russians invaded Poland, Khmelnytsky was not content with his pact with Alexis and entered into secret negotiations with the Swedes, who were also at war with Poland. He was about to conclude a treaty with the Swedes, which would have placed the Cossacks under Swedish rule when he died

About the translator

George Nafziger earned his BS from Miami University in 1971, his MBA from Miami University in 1976, and his Ph.D. in Military History from The Union Institute in 1999. He was commissioned as an Ensign USN in 1971 and served 4 years on active duty, including two tours to Vietnam aboard the USS Hull. In 1975 he left the regular Navy and joined the Reserves in 1977. He retired from the US Navy Reserves as a Captain in 1995.

Nafziger is a former director of the Napoleonic Society of America and the Napoleonic Alliance. He served on the board of directors of HMGS East.]

Nafziger is the owner of The Nafziger Collection publishing house, specializing in military history. As of 2013, it produces 385 different titles on military history ranging from the Middle Ages through the Korean War, with a heavy emphasis on the Wars of the French Revolution, the Napoleonic Wars, and World War II. As a publisher of obscure military works, he is constantly seeking authors with unpublished manuscripts on military history that are seeking a publisher.[2]

He worked in a US Department of State program known as ACOTA, where he trained African officers in peacekeeping operations from 2002 to 2012.

For more information on the Nafziger Collection please visit:

http://www.nafzigercollection.com/

PO Box 1522
West Chester, OH 45071-1522

For more information on Winged Hussar Publishing, LLC please visit us at:

https://www.wingedhussarpublishing.com

1525 Hulse Road, Unit 1
Point Pleasant, NJ 08742

We support many fine historical organizations, here is one:

The Council on America's Military Past, USA, Inc. (CAMP) is one of the leading national military history organizations dedicated to preserving, interpreting and sharing our military heritage.

Our purpose is to identify, memorialize, preserve and publicize America's military history including the structures and facilities used by our soldiers, the living conditions, customs and traditions of our men and women in uniform, and the progress and purpose of United States military organizations.

We produce two publication: Heliogram and JAMP as well as a yearly organizational Meeting

For membership information, please refer to the website:

www.campjamp.org

or contact Nick Reynolds, membership secretary at nereyn@earthlink.net

502 N. Norwood St
Arlington, VA 22203